RAISING FUNDS FO
LC243.A1 G3

P9-AGP-579

DATE DUE

JE 9 '04			

DEMCO 38-296

RAISING FUNDS FOR YOUR CHILD'S SCHOOL

RAISING FUNDS FOR YOUR CHILD'S SCHOOL

OVER SIXTY GREAT IDEAS FOR PARENTS AND TEACHERS

Cynthia Francis Gensheimer

WALKER AND COMPANY
New York

To
My husband, Joe
My children, Michael, Lydia, and Juliana
My parents, Beverly and Norman Francis
My grandmother Pauline Cohen
And to the memory of my grandmother Jennie Francis

Copyright © 1993 by Cynthia Francis Gensheimer

First published in the United States of America in 1993 by Walker Publishing
Company, Inc.

Published simultaneously in Canada by Thomas Allen & Son Canada, Limited,
Markham, Ontario

Library of Congress Cataloging-in-Publication Data
Gensheimer, Cynthia Francis
    Raising funds for your child's school : over sixty great ideas for
parents and teachers / Cynthia Francis Gensheimer.
        p.   cm.
    Includes bibliographical references (p.   ) and index.
    ISBN 0-8027-1281-9 —ISBN 0-8027-7411-3 (pbk.)
    1. Educational fund-raising—United States.   2. Home and school—
United States.   I. Title.
LB2336.G48   1993
379.1'3'0973—dc20   93-1709
                                                                CIP

Book design by Glen Edelstein

Printed in the United States of America

10   9   8   7   6   5   4   3   2   1

CONTENTS

ACKNOWLEDGMENTS

This book began as an outgrowth of my work with my own PTA, initially as cochair of the book fair at my children's school. When New York State sharply reduced state aid to local school districts, a group of us active in the PTA decided to explore new fund-raising ideas. Having previously lived in California, Virginia, and Connecticut, I have friends scattered throughout the country, and I began calling them to see how they raise money for their children's schools. After a few days of calling, I'd already learned a tremendous amount, and it occurred to me that I ought to continue my research and share my newfound knowledge by writing a book on this subject.

Eventually, I interviewed people from nearly every state in the country. My friends had given me names and phone numbers of parents in charge of fund-raisers at their children's schools. When I called to interview them, they were all extremely helpful and forthcoming. I concluded that many ran their fund-raisers with such efficiency and expertise that they could have been running corporations instead. In many cases, these women (for nearly all are women) were so busy balancing their work and volunteer efforts that they asked me to call after 10:00 P.M. or before 8:00 A.M., but they still found time to talk to me.

I'd like to thank the many people whom I interviewed and who sent me information about their fund-raising activities. These include: Mary Jane Ackroyd, Carol Adams, Marlene Adams, Mary Ellen Albarino, Lynda Baccoli, Andrea Bamrick, Margot Bean, Ann Beckerman, Kathleen Bennett, Ginny Blauvelt, Susie Blecker, Kathy Borges, Joan Brown, Jean Bundy,

Shirley Carlin, Lettice Carroll, Clara Cecil, Jo Cirelli, Karen Clark, Linna Cohen, Sydnye Cohen, Mary Colhoun, Barbara Corner, Lisabeth Crawford, Judy Dannes, Barbara Daugherty, Carol David, Marcia DeOteris, Jodi DeSantis, Gay Lee Einstein, Ellen Erne, Martha Fischer, Suzanne Fishkin, Barbara Fornaca, Lynn Fornadel, Carol Fransen, Patty Gehring, Dawn Gehrke, Bonnie Glick, Meryl Gordon, Sharon Gordon, Mara Green, Carla Greenberg, Jaricia Griess, Pauline Griess, Marcia Hahnenberger, Judy Hall, Jennifer Harris, Martha Harris, Jean Harrison, Dawn Heflin, Susie Herrera, Naomi Holmes, Sue Hornbeck, Jennifer Horton, Bailey and Jean Howard, Janet Johnson, Deborah Kahn, Peter Karpoff, Beth Kenagy, Lisa Kerchman, Ann Knudson, Bridget Krowe, Ellen Kuba, Jane Larke, Kitty Latowicki, Linda Lendman, Darlene Lexa, Roberta Licalzi, Debbie Lionetti, Alana Long, Bette Lo-Presti, Sue Lukatchik, MaryAnn MacLean, Karen Maher, Barbara Margulis, Marty Marinoff, Janet Martin, Helene McCabe, Dan McLaughlin, Noreen Moser, Sharel Neilland, Betsy Nelms, Joan Nurge, Rita O'Connor, Laurie Pearce, Bonnie Pearson, Christine Pellor, Laurie Plotch, Myszka Reeck, Rosemary Reeves, Fredda Regen, Susan Ricci, Joyce Richardson, Linda Ritchie, Kelly Robinson, Dora Rossi, Bill Russell, Lisa Ryan, Toby Schaffer, Barbara Seldin, Kathy Seldin, Arleen Sepulveda, Jim Skeen, Jan Smith, Dorothy Soranno, Karen Stapleton, Brenda Stockton-Hiss, Kim Stranick, Nancy Stuever, Kathy Sullivan, Paula Swain, Beth Tartaglia, Claire Thoms, Lois Tigay, Cathy Tobkin, Kip Toner, Andrea Tuccillo, Janet Van Syckle, Jamie Vroom, Jenna Walker, Lance Walker, Ruth Warren, Kathleen Watt, Sharon Wendorf, Joanie Wilcox, Diane Winkler, Barbara Wolf, and Judy Woodrich.

In writing the book, I drew heavily on experiences of actual schools throughout the country. When I read the manual put together by past chairs of the fun fair at Spring Hill Elementary School in McLean, Virginia, I first realized what a group of organized, dedicated, and energetic parents could accomplish. The terrific women from Nishuane School in Montclair, New Jersey, helped enormously, providing inspiration along with information on many fund-raisers.

Actual forms and letters supplied by those and the following schools have been adapted for use in the book: Clifton

Elementary School, Craig School, El Descanso, Glover School, Great Falls School, Hagan Spackenkill Elementary School, Hillside School, La Cañada Flintridge Educational Foundation, Meadows Elementary School, Monroe Elementary School, Reed School, Stirling Elementary School, Sunrise Valley Elementary School, and Webster Magnet School.

I owe special thanks to Kathy Borges, Sydnye Cohen, Judy Dannes, Marcia DeOteris, Patty Gehring, Dawn Gehrke, Judy Hall, Sue Hornbeck, Debra Kahn, Peter Karpoff, and Alana Long, who reviewed the manuscript and offered detailed, helpful suggestions for improvements. Sue Conger and Diane Winkler very kindly typed the first few chapters, and a good friend, Myra Schiffmann, edited them, which got me started in the right direction. My editor at Walker, Mary Kennan Herbert, was supportive and helpful throughout.

Most of all I thank my family. From childhood, I have had the constant support of parents and grandparents who gave me the confidence that I could accomplish what I set out to do. My children, Michael and Lydia, provided the initial inspiration for this book; I became active in the PTA because they loved my volunteering at their school. The newest member of the family, Juliana, was born a few hours after I finished the manuscript; she spent nine months in utero at the computer and was gracious enough to hold off her entrance into this world until I was ready to turn my attention to her. Finally, and most important, I thank my husband, Joe, whose guidance and advice were always forthcoming and whose willingness to share household responsibilities really made this book possible.

PREFACE

"My son loves gymnastics, and I really want to encourage him. Is it true that his school needs money to buy new playground equipment?"

"Kim's happiest when she's got her nose buried in a book. I want to be sure her school library has the support it needs to buy new titles."

As parents and teachers of elementary school children, all of us want the same thing. We want our schools to be the best they can be so our children can get the best possible education during their formative years. But frankly, that takes money. And at a time when states around the country are cutting back on funding for local school districts, we have reason for concern. Those cutbacks could mean larger class sizes, reductions in music and art instruction, fewer field trips, less money spent on athletic equipment and on books for the school library, and elimination of kindergarten and programs for the gifted and talented.

But the fact is, parents and teachers involved in local PTAs can do a lot to help the situation. With a little organization, determination, and luck, we can move beyond the bake sale to raise money for our schools—to the tune of thousands of dollars every year. Money that could mean new computers, gym equipment, music and art supplies, and books for the library. Money that could free up tax dollars to be spent on keeping teachers who might otherwise lose their jobs.

This book has been written to share successful, creative

ideas and tried-and-true methods for elementary school fund-raising. As a parent active in my own PTA, I know what it takes to run fund-raisers. I've talked to people around the country who've contributed fantastic ideas about running fund-raisers, big and small.

I believe that grass-roots action on behalf of local schools not only will benefit the school programs we want for our kids but will bring us together in our communities. What better way to get to know your neighbors than to work together to raise money for the school?

Both men and women have a great deal to contribute. Whether you're an ace at bookkeeping and volunteer to total up the receipts . . . or whether you've got a flair for publicity . . . or whether you bake the greatest pan of brownies in town, you have something important to offer. This book will show you how. And one look at your kids will tell you why.

Good luck!

INTRODUCTION:

How to Get Started

MAYBE YOUR PTO OR PTA OR ALUMNI ASSOCIATION IS TRYING to find new ways to raise money for your child's school, or maybe you're looking for ways to spruce up tried-and-true annual fund-raisers. Either way, this is the book for you. It's a step-by-step guide to school fund-raising, geared primarily to elementary schools—public, private, and parochial.

Each chapter includes detailed information on when to have the fund-raiser; whether to work with a company that specializes in running fund-raisers or run it in-house; what committees you'll need and the responsibilities of each; and what to do six months, two months, one month, and one week in advance of the event.

Parents and teachers who've run the various fund-raisers recount their experiences from nearly every state in the country. Most tell about fund-raising for public schools, but some tell about independent, private, or parochial schools, where they often bring in more than $100,000 per year for each school. If you need to raise tens of thousands of dollars for your school, read Chapters 4, 6, 9, and 10 to learn about the clothesline (rummage) sales, auctions, and social events that private schools have held for years.

In this book I describe a number of events that you might not think of primarily as fund-raisers: social events for school families, fun fairs, performances for children, ice cream socials, and spaghetti dinners, to name a few. It's up to you to decide how much to charge for them. You can charge a nominal fee, provide some of them free, or, if necessary, mark up the price to turn them into fund-raisers. See Chapter 7 to learn what a school in Virginia does to raise more than $10,000 from its fun fair every spring.

At the end of each chapter you'll find such practical information as the names and phone numbers of companies to work with, sample letters to send home to parents, and sample forms to use for your own accounting purposes. The letters and forms have been collected from a cross section of real elementary schools and are reproduced here with minor revisions. In most cases, I've substituted the name of the fictional "Lincoln Elementary School" for the actual school name, but where a letter or form is highly specific to a particular school, I've substituted a dash (_____) instead.

HOW MUCH CAN YOU EXPECT TO RAISE IN A YEAR?

How much you raise in a year depends on how aggressive you want to be about fund-raising and how affluent your community is. One 600-student school in New Hampshire raises $15,000 with one fund-raiser—a sale of candy, wrapping paper, and novelty gifts every fall. To make this single annual fund-raiser as profitable as possible, the PTA invites fund-raising companies to come to a meeting in the spring to bid on it. PTA Second Vice President Jodi DeSantis says: "This works out extremely well. Every company offers many benefits to us because of our volume of sales and the chance to have their reputation spread through the rest of the school district."

One 600-student public school in California, hard hit by budget cutbacks, raises $70,000 a year from direct donations, a readathon, a large rummage sale, a spring festival and auction, two book fairs, penny collections, and ongoing sales of "spirit clothing" (school T-shirts, sweatshirts, jackets, dresses, and so forth). The money that is raised pays for field trips, aides for all the classes, and the salaries of math, science, and art specialists.

Most PTAs are not expected to pay for such fundamentals

and hence need raise only a few thousand dollars annually. In that case, one or two low-key fund-raisers per year are plenty.

HOW TO MAKE THE MOST BY WORKING THE LEAST

Like looking for the least expensive restaurant with the best food, looking for the fund-raiser that's likely to be most profitable while requiring the least work is not an easy task. The best bets are probably readathons, walkathons, raffles, sales of wrapping paper or magazines, and direct donations from parents. If you're looking for a new idea that would be somewhat more difficult but manageable and likely to net over $1,000, try a sale of plants for Mother's Day, used sporting goods, or note cards the children have designed themselves.

In the accompanying chart, the types of fund-raisers discussed in each chapter are rated according to complexity and potential profitability. Complexity is determined by how much organization and volunteer time and effort a given fund-raiser entails, with ratings ranging from one to three asterisks:

    *   easiest
   **   moderately complex
  ***   substantially complex

The ratings for potential profitability are approximations only and are based on a school whose children come from middle-income homes. The number of dollar signs indicates how much an average school of 500 students could net from a well-run fund-raiser of a given type:

    $ less than $1,000
   $$ $1,000–$2,500
  $$$ $2,500–$8,000
 $$$$ more than $8,000

	COMPLEXITY	PROFITABILITY
Chapter 1 Walkathon/jogathon	*	$$$$

	COMPLEXITY	PROFITABILITY
Chapter 2		
Readathon/mathathon/spellathon/ knowledge-a-thon	★	$$$$
Chapter 3		
Book fair	★★	$$$
Chapter 4		
Clothesline sale	★★★	$$$$
Used sporting goods sale	★★	$$
Chapter 5		
Wrapping paper/candy/magazine sale	★	$$$
Mother's Day plant sale	★★	$$
Pie/pizza/submarine sandwich sale	★★	$$
Note card/calendar sale	★★	$
Videotape sale	★	$
Cookbook sale	★★	$$
Holiday shop	★★	$
Craft fair	★★	$
Family portrait sale	★	$$
School T-shirt sale	★	$$
School supply store	★★	$
Chapter 6		
Auction	★★★	$$$$
Chapters 7 and 8		
Fun fair	★★★	$$
Chapter 9		
Student/parent/teacher production	★★	$–$$
Movie	★	$
Family roller-skating	★	$
Family square dancing	★	$
All-adult social event	★★	$$
Spaghetti dinner	★★	$$
Pizza dinner	★	$

	COMPLEXITY	PROFITABILITY
Ice cream social	★	$
Dessert buffet	★	$
Pancake breakfast	★★	$$
Chapter 10		
Direct solicitation of parents	★	$$$
Selling ads in journals and school directories	★★	$$$
Grocery-store receipt program	★★	$$$
Food-label program	★★	$

"FUN-RAISERS"

Don't forget that fund-raisers serve a multiplicity of purposes. Not only can they raise money, but they can foster a sense of community and school spirit. Many schools call their fund-raisers "fun-raisers." Peter Karpoff, treasurer of an eighty-eight-student private school in Silver Spring, Maryland, puts it this way: "The Spring Fair raised something over $8,000, a pretty high per-family figure. But the real payoff is not just the money. The kids and parents all have such a nice time. The fair itself is fun, but the parent involvement in getting ready for it is also an important experience in community-building."

Nothing beats a fun fair (carnival) in generating enthusiasm among children. Other fund-raisers that raise school spirit include all the events listed in Chapter 9, Food and Entertainment. In terms of making a contribution to the community, clothesline sales (schoolwide garage sales) probably win first prize, since they allow used clothing and household goods to be recycled and sold at reasonable prices.

HOW MANY FUND-RAISERS SHOULD YOU HAVE EACH YEAR?

You need to set a goal for how much money you'd like to raise in a school year and then decide how to go about it. Parents hate to feel that they're being asked for money every time they look in their children's backpacks or walk into school. For this reason, some schools sponsor just one fund-raiser every year—an auction, a joint sale of wrapping paper and gift foods, a readathon, or a walkathon. Other schools feature a major fund-raiser in the fall and another in the spring, and some schools offer fund-raisers throughout the year with the understanding that parents will support those that appeal to them the most.

It makes sense for some fund-raisers to be annual events, so participants can count on supporting them. If parents and teachers know, for instance, that the school is going to sell wrapping paper every fall or bedding plants every spring, they will hold off making those purchases elsewhere. If the school holds a sale of used sporting goods at the same time every year, people will know to save their used skates and skis and wait to make this year's purchases at the sale. On the other hand, variety is good also, so you might want to have one or two annual fund-raisers and then try something different, such as publishing a cookbook one year and hosting varied social events every year.

WHAT TO DO WHEN PARENTS OBJECT TO FUND-RAISING

Some parents find the whole notion of school fund-raising distasteful, objecting to paying a premium for goods that they might not even want to buy. You can keep this criticism to a minimum by making sure to sell something desirable: plants at Mother's Day, a cookbook, school T-shirts, books or crafts right before the holidays, or citrus fruit.

Of course, an alternative is not to sell anything. You can turn to a different type of fund-raiser—a fun fair, raffle, auction, or walkathon, or an all-adult social affair to which parents must pay admission. These events are all described in this book.

Some schools take a more radical approach—promising to eliminate all fund-raisers for a year on a trial basis. If they manage to reach their fund-raising goal solely by soliciting direct donations from parents, they agree not to have any fund-raisers the following year either. For tips on how to solicit funds directly from parents, see Chapter 10. Chapter 10 also covers the ways that businesses help schools—by donating cash, computers and other equipment, volunteers, and much more.

Laurie Plotch of Scottsdale, Arizona, has her own way of supporting her child's school: "I don't like the PTAs selling things we don't need at inflated prices. And what's worse is they get our kids all jazzed up with promises of great prizes. I have come to my own solution on this. Every year, I find out what the school needs and I donate money directly into that cause instead of buying cheese and crackers. This year the library needed some new paperback books. It cost $50 to donate the set, but they put my kid's name in the school newspaper for the donation and the school got 100 percent of the value."

Many parents would agree with Laurie as far as their children are concerned. They object to their children being asked to sell things, particularly if the kids get rewarded by an array of inexpensive trinkets depending on how much merchandise they sell. In fact, the National PTA states that a fund-raising project should "involve children only as an outgrowth of regular schoolwork or as a constructive use of leisure time."

HOW TO RECRUIT AND KEEP VOLUNTEERS

Although some fund-raisers are so simple that they can be run single-handedly or with just a few volunteers, most rely on a fair number of volunteers. With most parents working these days, how can you succeed in recruiting volunteers?

First, select someone to oversee the recruitment of volunteers for all activities, and put a different person in charge of recruiting and scheduling volunteers for each specific fund-raiser. Get a list of new parents at the beginning of the year, and have veteran parents call each family to welcome them and answer any questions. Invite them (and all other parents) to a tea or informational meeting at which you describe your needs for volunteers and have sign-up sheets on hand for each fund-raiser. Ask the people who will chair each major event to be present, too.

Send fliers home to all parents at the beginning of the year asking for volunteers for all the fund-raisers. When it's time to assign particular tasks or time slots to individuals, make sure that you call each and every person who signed up to help.

People feel excluded, rejected, and angry if they've never been taken up on their offers to help.

Maintain records year-to-year of who's helped out with a particular activity. Chances are that someone who's worked at the book fair one year enjoys that sort of thing and will agree to do it again.

If you don't get enough volunteers through the sign-up sheets, ask people directly. Often parents will agree to help out if asked by another parent. At some schools, parents aren't asked *whether* they'll help out, but rather *how* they'll help out. A school in Connecticut has a gigantic "gourmet sale"—a glorified bake sale—and every year each family gets a call asking what it will be contributing.

"I used the school directory and called every parent asking them to volunteer their time," reports Jaricia Griess of Michigan. "When I needed a lot of volunteers, I recruited three other moms to make evening phone calls. If we didn't ask directly, no one would ever help."

When volunteers show up for work, make them feel welcome. Greet them at the door, introduce them to other volunteers, and give them specific responsibilities. Since the same small group of parents often does a lot of the work at the PTA, they tend to become good friends and can be perceived as a "clique," unwittingly making outsiders feel excluded. Make sure to bend over backward to be friendly, to delegate authority, and to ask different people to be in charge of activities so the same small group isn't always doing everything.

Make volunteers official by giving them name tags. Some schools even have matching bandannas, aprons, or buttons for volunteers to wear. These items get saved and are used repeatedly.

Don't have more volunteers than the job requires. When people volunteer their time, they like to feel it's really needed. Everyone has given up valuable time to be there, and some may even have had to pay a baby-sitter. You might offer baby-sitting services for preschoolers, so their parents can more easily come and help out. One parent could supervise the children, or you could even hire a baby-sitter.

Make sure to say thank you! You can give each volunteer a token gift—a long-stemmed carnation from a plant sale or a free book from a book fair. Write each volunteer a thank-you note, and have a thank-you tea or lunch. At a primary school in Connecticut, the principal hosts a coffee every year in June to thank all the year's volunteers. She gives each volunteer a personal thank-you and a long-stemmed rose. The teachers supply the baked goods as their way of saying thank you.

PICK THE RIGHT PERSON FOR THE JOB

Utilize the talents of the people at your school and in the community. If someone is a graphic artist, ask him or her to design a logo for your school T-shirts, invitations to an auction, or a program for a fun fair. Find someone with a head for numbers to handle the financial end of your fund-raisers. Seek out someone with an artistic bent to do decorations, and someone who can write to create press releases.

When it comes to tapping specific talents, you probably have to ask rather than rely on someone knowing exactly what you need and volunteering on his or her own. In conjunction with its book fair, one school hired a different entertainer—folksinger, storyteller, or magician—every year for a family performance in the evening. When someone learned that the father of a third-grader had been a professional entertainer, she asked him to do the program one year. Not only did the PTA save $400, but the father did an outstanding job.

Don't forget to reach out to all working parents. People who work during the day can do behind-the-scenes work such as writing press releases after hours, and if events are scheduled in the evening or on weekends, working parents can volunteer more conveniently. "One Halloween, our 'room daddies' built and manned the haunted house," says Kathy Borges. "From then on they got a lot more involved."

Someone needs to be in charge of fund-raising in general for the PTA or PTO and is often given the title "vice president for ways and means" (or "for fund-raising"). He or she has the responsibility of coordinating all annual fund-raising—planning what fund-raisers to have when and recruiting people to be in charge of each activity. This person must clearly work closely with the school principal to plan events that she and the faculty support. At most private schools, a school employee oversees fund-raising.

Generally, you need one person to chair each fund-raiser, although for a difficult-to-run event such as an auction or clothesline sale you probably need two people to act as cochairs. Some schools have their chairs serve for two years. One person assists the chair the first year, automatically becoming chair the next year, with her heir apparent helping her that year.

Each fund-raiser requires a different set of subcommittees, described in detail in the chapters that follow. In general, at a minimum, you'll need to find people to be in charge of publicity, finance, decorations, volunteers, and liaison with the principal, teachers, and any company through which you're working.

COMMUNICATION

No fund-raiser will be successful unless you keep parents, teachers, and the principal informed about the activity and their respective roles in it. Having a good PTA/PTO newsletter is important, but so is sending fliers home and memos to the teachers letting them know what's coming up. Ask someone in the cafeteria to post reminder notices about fund-raisers on the monthly menu. If there is a marquee or billboard in front of your school, use it. Send press releases to the local newspaper— it's always looking for stories. The more often parents read and hear about a fund-raiser, the more apt they are to remember to participate.

Give people enough time to follow through. Remember that teachers don't always send notices home as soon as they get them, and children don't always remember to show them to their parents. Always give people a week or two to send in their orders for T-shirts, recipes for a cookbook, money collected from a walkathon, or whatever.

After the fund-raiser, make sure to let everyone know how successful it was. When the school spends the money you've raised, let parents know where the funds have gone.

Fund-raisers can be more successful if you announce in advance that money raised is being earmarked for a specific purpose—a new playground, for instance. Sell T-shirts with a design of the playground on them. Ask each child to collect pennies, and see if you can cover the gym floor with them. To raise money for a new sound system for the auditorium, charge admission to a children's talent show, teacher or parent follies, or a children's play or concert.

KEEP GOOD RECORDS

Especially when it comes to fund-raisers that are annual events, keeping good records from year to year is imperative. Just think of the amount of work you can save by keeping on file fliers that you sent to parents, memos to teachers, signs that you posted at school, and simple reminders of what to do and when to do it.

Imagine how much easier your job would be as first-time chair of an event if you were handed a file from your predecessor containing a report of what he or she had done the year before. The best-run PTAs and PTOs ask the people who chair their fund-raisers to submit reports a few weeks after the event. These reports cover the jobs that had to be done, time schedules, planning and setting up, items purchased and a list of suppliers, names of people dealt with, and expenses.

LEGAL ADVICE

When in doubt about the legality of a fund-raiser the PTA is considering, consult an attorney. (Perhaps a parent who is a lawyer will volunteer advice.) Be sure you understand state law before having a raffle or a bingo night, and call the local health department to check state regulations before selling food at school. If the PTA plans to sponsor an activity such as roller-skating that could be dangerous, check the PTA's insurance policy to see if it's necessary to pay for an insurance rider. PTAs and their presidents have even been sued for accidents that have occurred on playgrounds that they've helped to build on school property.

Parents might ask whether purchases they make at school

fund-raisers qualify for income tax deductions as charitable contributions. As a general rule, only amounts spent above the "fair market value" of an item can be deducted. In other words, if someone spent $10 for a mug worth $4, he or she could deduct $6 as a charitable contribution. If the mug was worth $10, however, no deduction would be allowed.

If individuals donate items to the school, they can take tax deductions for the value of what they've donated. If you accept donations for a clothesline sale, you should provide donors with receipts that they can use for tax purposes. If merchants donate goods from their inventory, they can claim as a charitable contribution the amount of their actual cost. Send all donors thank-you notes and receipts. The IRS has a fund-raising hotline (202-343-8900) that you can call with questions. You might want to request the following IRS publications:

Publication 526   "Charitable Contributions"
Publication 561   "Determining the Value of Donated Property"
Publication 1391   "Deductibility of Payments Made to Charities Conducting Fund-Raising Events"

In some states, items sold by the PTA are subject to state sales tax. California recently enacted a "snack tax," and many PTAs found themselves owing the state hundreds of dollars on proceeds from candy sales.

OFFICIAL PTA POSITION ON FUND-RAISING

Don't make fund-raising the sole, or even the primary, activity of the PTA or PTO. The National PTA publishes a leaflet, "Funding PTA Projects," which states: "Fund-raising is not a primary function of the PTA. Funds are raised as necessary to carry out PTA work. The real working capital of a PTA lies not in its treasury, but in its members' energy, resourcefulness, and determination to promote the well-being of children and youth." It suggests that each PTA sponsor one annual fund-raising project and that the funds be used to finance speakers and refreshments at PTA functions, attendance at state and national PTA meetings, and publication of a PTA newsletter.

It explicitly discourages PTAs from giving money or equipment to schools, since PTAs in more affluent districts can raise much more than their poorer neighbors. The leaflet goes on to state that "a PTA renders a greater service by securing public support for education and other community needs than by making gifts to the school."

SCHOOL BOARD POLICY

Some school boards set policy on school fund-raising. In one of the country's most affluent communities, Greenwich, Connecticut, the school board set a policy to restrict private donations. The board reaffirmed the notion that public money should support public education. Any gift of more than $5,000 must now be approved by the school board. In general, the board decided to accept gifts to expand existing programs but turn down those that might change the focus of a program or initiate a new one. Board members also voted to prohibit door-to-door solicitation by students.

GETTING STARTED

Browse through this book to get an idea of whether you're interested in having a readathon, an auction, a sale of some sort, or a fun fair. Once you've decided on an activity, read the nitty-gritty details that will help you plan and execute it successfully. Remember that most young kids love to see their parents volunteering at school, that your own children will benefit in many ways from your involvement, and that you'll meet new friends among parents and teachers and discover talents you never knew you had.

CHAPTER ONE

ATHLETIC MARATHONS: WALKATHONS, JOGATHONS, AND FIELD DAYS

"I REALLY LIKED THE JOGATHON," SAYS NINE-YEAR-OLD JIMMY Warren of North Carolina. "It felt really good that I did more than twenty laps and got a trophy. It was for a good cause." The president of the PTA at Jimmy's school is just as enthusiastic: "Kids love it, teachers love it, and it is the simplest fund-raiser you can have. There's no product to sell." The school of about 600 students in Raleigh, North Carolina, raised $14,000 with its first-ever jogathon.

This school worked through a company to do its jogathon, but schools that organize theirs in-house also make a great deal of money with a minimum amount of effort. Carla Greenberg of Marblehead, Massachusetts, coordinated walkathons at her local elementary school for the past two years. "The most difficult part of this fund-raiser is adding up the money and making the deposit," she says. The walkathon at her school of 300 students raised about $6,500 the first year and $4,500 the second year.

"Kids get involved and have fun," reports Barbara Fornaca of Torrance, California. "The jogathon takes great organization, but it's over FAST and has been the best fund-raiser we've ever had. One hundred percent goes straight to the PTA and therefore the kids."

Throughout this chapter I use a walkathon as an example. The material can easily be adapted to any other type of athletic marathon, be it one in which children jog, skip rope, or participate in field-day activities. (To learn about academic marathons—reading, math, spelling, and knowledge-a-thons—refer to Chapter 2.)

WHAT IS A WALKATHON?

The concept of a walkathon is familiar: children solicit pledges of a certain monetary amount per lap, walk as many laps as they can, and then collect on their pledges. Donors usually have the option of making a flat contribution instead of pledging per lap. Often, the school places a limit on the total number of laps that a child can walk (and charge for).

WHEN SHOULD YOU HAVE A WALKATHON?

If this is to be your only fund-raiser of the year, you might have to schedule your walkathon for the fall to generate the year's funds. In places where children are cooped up indoors all winter, though, a walkathon can be a perfect celebration of springtime. A spring walkathon works well also as a second large fund-raiser, complementing a fall sale of merchandise— books, wrapping paper, or crafts.

Whatever time of year you choose, select a rain date. If it rains on the rain date, have the walkathon in the gym.

Your principal and the PTA have to decide whether to have the walkathon during school hours or over a weekend or on a weekday after school. When walkathons are held during the school day, each class typically walks for twenty or thirty minutes, so the amount of lost class time is minimal. In fact, a walkathon can be considered a field day or physical education class. Participation during school hours is usually very high, so that's the optimal time to host the walkathon if you want to raise a large sum of money. For example, 80 percent of students at the Marblehead, Massachusetts, school participated in its walkathon, which was held during the school day.

By contrast, Kathy Borges of Somerset, Massachusetts, notes that her school of 260 elementary students had a turnout of only fifty for its Saturday-morning walkathon. And in Seattle, Washington, Naomi Holmes reports that one school holds its walkathon after school. A little under half the students participated last year. (Even at that, the 225 children who did walk raised $4,000.)

HOW DO YOU MAKE THE WALKATHON FESTIVE?

Decorate the course, play music, and invite parents to help and/or cheer. Some parents even like to walk with their children, although not for pledges.

Give snacks after the walking. One school offered orange slices outdoors. At another school, a potato chip manufacturer supplied free picnic lunches, and at a third school the room parents sent in pretzels and cupcakes, which the children ate in their classrooms. If the walkathon is held after school hours, and if you have enough parent volunteers, cap it off with a potluck supper, chili feed, or pizza party.

Choose a theme. In Seattle, one school used the theme "Walking Around the World" and "Coming Home to America" for chili afterward. Naomi Holmes says that the volunteers "hung flags of different countries at the corners of the course, and the kids had passports to be stamped for keeping track of their laps." In keeping with this theme, you could give the walkers buttons or T-shirts that said, "I walked around the world with _____ school."

SHOULD YOU WORK WITH A COMPANY?

There are a few companies that will organize your walkathon for you. They'll come in and kick off the event with a professional assembly for the students at which they generate enthusiasm by explaining the program and showing off incentive prizes. In addition, they'll supply a how-to-manual, letters to parents and sponsors, and the forms needed to keep track of laps walked. Depending on the company, an employee might come to oversee operations on the day of the walkathon.

Working through a company instead of running an in-house program reduces the amount of volunteer time required. The company handles all billing, using computers to bill the sponsors by mail, so children do not need to collect in person. In exchange, the company keeps a substantial share of the donated funds. After paying for commissions and all other expenses, schools typically net 50 to 70 percent of contributions. The companies in this business claim that schools raise so much more through them that, even after paying these commissions, the institutions net substantially more than they would make on their own.*

The monetary results of these company-run jogathons are impressive. For example, the 375 girls at a parochial high school in a New York suburb cleared $14,000 one year at a company-run walkathon. Those opposed to working with the companies argue, however, that the work can easily be done in-house, that the companies' share of the intake is hefty, and that they use high-pressure sales tactics to motivate children. The remainder of this chapter is a guide to doing your own walkathon. After reading it, you can judge for yourself how you'd like to do yours.

SHOULD YOU OFFER INCENTIVE PRIZES?

Offering some sort of incentive prizes can generate school spirit, make the children feel proud of their accomplishments, and at the same time motivate them to solicit pledges and walk many laps.

*Three companies that organize walkathons and jogathons are: AMER-A-THON 1-919-772-8057, CompuThon 1-800-327-0322, and Sunshine State Funding Corporation 1-813-576-3696.

A California school gives children school buttons to wear while getting sponsors, school pencils when they return their sponsor sheets, school cups filled with a drink when they finish jogging, and prizes depending on how much money they actually collect. Organizers of this event have found that giving prizes when children turn in their money provides a strong incentive for them to collect the pledges—the least enjoyable part of the event.

Other schools have run successful walkathons without offering any prizes at all or by offering prizes, but less expensive ones: school banners, buttons, or silver dollars.

HOW SHOULD CHILDREN GET PLEDGES?

Children are usually told to ask relatives, friends, and neighbors to sponsor them, but at the same time most schools discourage children from going door-to-door, and many employers forbid parents from soliciting contributions at work. To make it easy to request donations, your PTA can bill donors the way companies do. One company supplies students with mailers—form letters to send to potential donors asking if they'll sponsor a particular student (and if so, to circle the contribution per lap). The mailers are two-sided, so that donors simply refold, staple, and mail them back to the school. Another company asks students to submit names and addresses of sponsors to them. In both cases, the companies bill sponsors after the walkathon or jogathon.

HOW CAN YOU KEEP TRACK OF COMPLETED LAPS?

Most commonly, schools use rubber bands. Volunteers stand at the finish line and pass out a rubber band to each child as he or she completes a lap. The child puts the rubber band on his or her wrist and counts the total at the end. Alternatively, children wear paper sneakers (or passports) around their necks and have holes punched as they finish each lap. Yet another approach is to have volunteers stand at the finish line with class lists and clipboards and check off laps as each student goes by.

At one school, one parent from each classroom keeps track of the kids from that class, all of whom are wearing stickers of the same bright color to differentiate them from children in other classes. As each child completes another lap, the parent makes a mark on the child's sticker, and at the end of the jogathon, the parent removes the sticker and places it right on the child's sponsor sheet. This eliminates some paperwork and ensures that the sponsor sheets are immediately ready to be sent home for collection.

HOW CAN A WALKATHON BE USED AS A TEACHING TOOL?

Teachers can use a walkathon as a springboard for applying math concepts learned in the classroom. In the youngest classes, teachers can discuss who has walked the most laps, how many more laps Sarah walked than Charlie, and so on. The older children can answer questions such as, "If you can walk four laps in fifteen minutes, how many laps can you walk in an hour?" "If each lap is one-fifth of a mile long and you walk fifteen laps, how many miles have you walked?" "If you have pledges totaling $16 per lap and you walk twenty laps, how much money do you raise?" In the front entryway, teachers can graph contributions received by the various classes or laps completed by classes, teachers, or top walkers. If you are mailing requests to donors around the country, you can keep track of the states from which pledges arrive.

HOW CAN YOU GENERATE ENTHUSIASM AMONG STAFF AND PARENTS?

Get the full backing of the principal, involve teachers, and motivate parents. Teachers who are excited about the walkathon spread their enthusiasm to the children. Send a note to the teachers asking for their help and offering the above suggestions of ways to work the walkathon into their teaching. Ask them to walk themselves, not necessarily for pledges. Let parents know what the money will be used for and how it will help their children.

HOW CAN YOU ENSURE A SAFE DAY FOR ALL?

You don't want anybody to get hurt—injured, overtired, or overheated. For this reason, many schools sponsor walkathons rather than jogathons, and most have a school nurse present just in case someone does get injured. Particularly if it's going to be a hot day, students are usually offered water to drink during the walkathon and juice or water afterward as well. Parents even squirt hot students with water during the jogathon at one California school.

HOW CAN YOU INCLUDE HANDICAPPED STUDENTS?

Jenna Walker of Columbus, Ohio, says, "Handicapped students participated in our walkathon by serving refreshments, punching cards, doing errands, and cheering the other walkers. They got pledges of flat dollar amounts."

STEP-BY-STEP PLANNING AND PREPARATION

Stage One (Six Months Before)

THE COMMITTEE

The chair of the walkathon should form a committee, finding people to head the following subcommittees:

volunteers
setup, cleanup, decorations, and beverages
publicity
finance
prizes

Hold a preliminary meeting of the committee to formulate a game plan. Decide when you'd like to have the walkathon, whether you want to offer incentive prizes, and if so how to structure the incentives. Select a theme.

THE CHAIR

Meet with the school principal to get her backing and approval and to select a date and a rain date. (Do not hold your walkathon on a Monday, since teachers need the day before the event to remind students that pledge sheets must be turned in the next day.) Ask the principal to let the teachers know the walkathon is coming up so they can begin to think about how to incorporate it into their teaching. Discuss school policy on whether:

> it's okay to have the walkathon during school hours
>
> the program should be explained to the kids during an assembly, by teachers in their classrooms, or just through letters sent home
>
> it's okay to play music and invite parents
>
> children need parental permission to walk
>
> a nurse should be present at the walkathon
>
> it's okay to offer incentive prizes
>
> a short celebration can follow the actual walk

PRIZES

If you are going to offer incentive prizes such as school T-shirts, buttons, or trophies, begin shopping for them.

Stage Two (Three to Six Weeks Before)

THE COMMITTEE

The committee should meet again to discuss strategy and problems. Decide how you'll keep track of completed laps, what kind of decorations you want, what kind of music to play, and what kind of food and drink to serve.

THE CHAIR

Touch base with the principal. Select the walking course— around a track or playground. Most elementary schools lay out a course that is one-eighth to one-fourth of a mile long.

VOLUNTEERS

Have the teachers select time slots for the day of the walkathon. Try to have all classes at each grade level walk together. Once you have time slots, you can send the schedule home with the children as part of a letter asking for volunteers. That way, parents can volunteer when their own children are walking. Time slots of an hour and a half work well for volunteers. Make sure that you have plenty of volunteers on hand. You don't want kids waiting to be logged in at the end of each lap.

SETUP, CLEANUP, DECORATIONS, AND BEVERAGES

Ask a few people to help you with the tasks on the day of the walkathon. Begin getting the decorations ready. Decide how you'll mark off the course. (You might just ask the gym teacher if you can borrow some orange cones the day of the walkathon.) Make arrangements for the beverages—whether you'll be serving water or trying to get drink mix donated from a fast-food restaurant. Gather or make whatever you'll need to keep track of laps completed (rubber bands, paper shoes and yarn . . .).

PUBLICITY

Write and photocopy all the required forms and letters. You will need:

> letters to parents/teachers/sponsors explaining the walkathon
>
> letter asking for parent volunteers
>
> forms for children to record names of sponsors and amounts pledged per lap
>
> letters to parents and sponsors about payment of pledges
>
> notice to be sent home a week after the walkathon reminding parents to send in pledges
>
> four manila envelopes per teacher—one for collection of pledge sheets and three for money (write teacher's name on each)

form for tallying funds received by classroom

Samples of letters and forms appear at the end of the chapter.

FINANCE

Ask a few people if they will help you collect the money each day as it comes in, count it, and make the bank deposits. At a 300-student school, three mothers did all the bookkeeping and money collecting. Arrange to have a "For deposit only" stamp, coin rolls, and bank deposit bags.

PRIZES

Purchase any prizes that you are going to give.

Stage Three (One Week Before)

Kick off the walkathon with a fifteen-minute assembly if you wish. Explain how the walkathon will work, and show the prizes the children can earn.

Send teachers the memo asking for their help. Send children home with pledge sheets and letters to parents and sponsors. Give each teacher a manila envelope with his name on it, so that he'll have it to store pledge sheets as they're returned.

Ask room parents to arrange to send in whatever food you decide to serve.

Stage Four (the Day Before)

Remind teachers of their time slots, and ask them to remind students to bring in their pledge forms.

Stage Five (the Day of the Walkathon)

FINANCE

Make sure that you have collected each teacher's manila envelope containing pledge sheets.

SETUP, CLEANUP, DECORATIONS, AND BEVERAGES

Decorate the track, and delineate it with orange cones. Set up the beverage table, and fill enough cups for one group. Make sure you have a trash can for the used cups. Set up for any music you're going to have. Have your logging system in place (rubber bands, sneakers and hole punch, stickers, or class rosters).

PRIZES

Set up prizes on a table so they'll be handy when it's time to pass them out.

VOLUNTEERS

Greet volunteers as they arrive, and have them fill out name tags. Assign them tasks: one or two at the beverage table, a few placed strategically along the track, and the rest at the finish line. Start each class by giving the kids instructions. Ask them not to run, and tell them to make sure to check in with a volunteer upon completing each lap. This is their responsibility. To begin, call off names one by one so that the children don't stampede at the start. At the conclusion of the twenty- or thirty-minute period, blow a whistle. Have students line up in alphabetical order by class so that you can record laps walked by each student. Thank the students and their teachers. Award any prizes, and serve the refreshments. On to the next group!

THE COMMITTEE

At the end of the day, clean up and record on the pledge forms the number of laps each child walked. (You can even have volunteers at work recording this information during the walk-athon as each class finishes, assuming that you have enough volunteers.) Give each teacher a thank-you letter and the pledge forms of children in his class, along with the accompanying letter to parents and sponsors.

Stage Six (a Few Days After)

Distribute the manila collection envelopes to the teachers. Then stop by their classes on a daily basis to collect the money. As it comes in each day, keep track of the totals by student and by class, if you want to. In any event, keep track of your running total, and make daily bank deposits. Return the empty envelopes to the teachers the next day when you go to collect again. A week after the walkathon, send home the reminder notice about turning in collected pledges.

Stage Seven (Two Weeks After)

You're all done! Thank the volunteers with notes, phone calls, or a party, and send a letter home thanking all participants and reporting your success. Have a meeting of the whole committee at which subcommittee chairs turn in their reports and you discuss what worked and what didn't and how to do things better the next time.

Dear Parents:

We'll be having our Walkathon on Tuesday, November 1. You are invited to come watch, cheer, or even walk if you'd like to. We also need lots of volunteers to help out. If you'd like to volunteer, please return this sheet to school. We've listed the schedule below to help you plan your visit.

9:00 A.M.– 9:30 A.M.:	kindergarten
9:45 A.M.–10:15 A.M.:	first grade
10:30 A.M.–11:00 A.M.:	second grade
11:00 A.M.–11:30 A.M.:	third grade
1:00 P.M.– 1:30 P.M.:	fourth grade
1:45 P.M.– 2:15 P.M.:	fifth grade

If you have any questions, please call _____ at _____ .

The Walkathon Committee

* *

Yes, I'd like to volunteer for:

☐ Shift 1: 8:45 A.M.–10:00 A.M.

☐ Shift 2: 10:00 A.M.–11:30 A.M.

☐ Shift 3: 12:45 P.M.–2:30 P.M.

Name _____

Phone _____

Thank You!!

Lincoln School Walkathon

Dear Students, Parents, and Friends:

The Lincoln School Second Annual Walkathon will be held on Tuesday, November 1. We will follow the same format as last year. Here is a review of the timetable of events.

First, the children will be given pledge sheets and asked to gather names of sponsors (people who will pledge so much money for each time the child walks a lap around a predetermined school path). Children are asked to get names of close friends, neighbors, and relatives and are not encouraged to go door-to-door to obtain pledges.

With the cooperation and assistance of the classroom teachers and administrators, each class will be allowed thirty minutes to walk. We believe this is an excellent opportunity for the students to be directly involved in raising funds for their own benefit. Also, there is no middleman involved. All profits will go directly to the school and, therefore, the students! Your participation and support of this endeavor is most important, because it means that we all want the same thing for our children. The very best education possible!!!

On _____ , your child will be bringing home his/her pledge sheet. These pledge sheets must be returned by _____ , in order for your child to participate (your signature is required), and so that the paperwork involved can be completed.

The Walkathon will be held on Tuesday, November 1 as stated. Rain date is _____ . Your child should wear comfortable sneakers.

By _____ , the children's pledge sheets will be returned to them, with confirmation of laps completed. All pledges must be returned to the school by _____ .

Thank you in advance for your cooperation.

The Walkathon Committee

Lincoln School Walkathon

Dear Teachers:

It is time for our Second Annual Walkathon. Money raised by the
Walkathon will help to fund various activities that the PTA already
sponsors, such as cultural arts and school improvements. Money will
also be used to fill the gaps caused by cuts to the budget.

We cannot have a successful Walkathon without your help. On the day
of the Walkathon, we ask that you take care of logging your children's
laps. You will be provided with a log sheet that has the children's
names and a space for the laps as they are completed.

It would be most helpful if you could talk about the Walkathon in class
when the pledge sheets first come out. The Walkathon can be used to
generate school spirit, and as a tool to incorporate age-appropriate
math-related exercises into a total school experience.

Thank you for your help. Further instructions will be forthcoming.

                              The Walkathon Committee

Dear Students and Parents:

Attached you will find your pledge sheets for our Second Annual Walkathon. It is time to start gathering pledges to help our school be the best it can be! We really expect every student to participate. WE NEED YOUR SUPPORT!!!

Remember, you should not go door-to-door to solicit pledges. Ask only close friends, neighbors, and relatives to pledge. Don't forget to thank everyone who pledges their support!! If people don't wish to make a pledge, they may make a donation in any amount, which will be collected at this time. A donation will be greatly appreciated.

Also, attached is a sponsor information sheet that ALL PLEDGERS should read. Make sure they realize that last year an average kindergartner walked six laps of the path in thirty minutes and that a pledge of $3 per lap for a student that age would cost $18. Also last year, an average third-grader walked eight laps in thirty minutes, so a pledge of $3 per lap would cost $24. They may wish to pledge a lesser amount. Make sure when your children are getting their pledges that they let the sponsor read the information sheet.

Below is a timetable that you can cut out and post (perhaps on the refrigerator) so you can remember all the important dates regarding the Walkathon.

Pledge sheets go home with students on _____ .

All pledge sheets MUST be returned by _____ .

WALKATHON is on Tuesday, November 1!!!

Rain date for Walkathon is _____ .

All monies MUST be returned to school by _____ .

Let's do our best to make this a successful Walkathon!!!

Thanks for your support!
The Walkathon Committee

LINCOLN SCHOOL

STUDENTS

ARE YOU READY?

WHAT DO I DO?

Visit your friends, neighbors, and relatives with your sponsor sheet.

WHY AM I DOING THIS?

You are earning money for your school for fine arts programs, field trips, supplemental enrichment equipment, and supplies.

WHAT IS A SPONSOR?

Any friend, neighbor, or relative who signs your sponsor sheet to support this activity.

WHAT IS A PLEDGE?

Money promised in return for laps completed.

HOW DO I GET PLEDGES?

Ask your sponsor if he or she would like to pledge ten cents, twenty-five cents, fifty cents per lap you complete. Some may want to make a contribution independent of laps. Have them fill in the spaces provided on your sponsor sheet, and let them know you will collect the money after you have completed your laps.

HOW MANY LAPS CAN I RUN?

You may run up to twenty-five laps.

Lincoln School Walkathon
Sponsor Information

Dear Sponsor:

The students of Lincoln School are trying to raise money to supplement field trips, in-school cultural events, equipment, and other necessities. We are having our Second Annual Walkathon during school hours on Tuesday, November 1.

We are asking for your help! Each student will have thirty minutes to walk laps around our school path. An average kindergartner can probably walk around the path six times in thirty minutes. An average third-grader can walk around the path eight times. Could you pledge an amount per lap to help us out? Any amount will be most appreciated. Below are some examples of pledges:

50¢ per lap × 6 laps = $3 (× 8 laps = $4)
$1 per lap × 6 laps = $6 (× 8 laps = $8)
$2 per lap × 6 laps = $12 (× 8 laps = $16)
$3 per lap × 6 laps = $18 (× 8 laps = $24)

Please note that last year third-graders walked anywhere from four to eleven laps in their thirty minutes. Fifth-graders walked anywhere from eight to eleven laps in their allotted time. These are about the best guidelines we can give as there is a great variation due to the individual child's stamina. Please pledge according to your child's ability.

If you do not wish to make a pledge, a donation in any amount will be greatly appreciated.

We thank you in advance for your support of this project.

Sincerely,
The Walkathon Committee

SAMPLE REMINDER NOTICE

Dear Parents:

Just a reminder that all Walkathon pledge sheets MUST be in by _____ . Your child will NOT be able to walk without YOUR SIGNATURE on the pledge sheet. Please help us to make this a successful project.

Thank you,
The Walkathon Committee

LINCOLN SCHOOL WALKATHON
Pledge Sheet

PURPOSE: The proceeds from this Walkathon will benefit our fine-arts programs, field trips, and supplemental enrichment equipment and supplies.

Pledge per Lap	or Contribution	Sponsor's Name	Address	Phone No.	Amount Due (Pledge x Laps)	Amount Paid

Student's Name_____ Room_____
Total_____

Parent's
Signature_____

My child may participate in the Walkathon on Tuesday, November 1 (rain date of_____).

MAXIMUM NUMBER OF LAPS IS 25. DO NOT REMOVE PERFORATED EDGES!

Dear Volunteers:

1. Each student will wear on his or her back a sticker color coded by class. The volunteer will make a tally mark for each lap completed and at the end of the event put the sticker on the student's pledge sheet. The volunteer will hand each student a ticket redeemable for refreshments. We are hoping for two to three parents per class to help with this.

2. We will need one parent to "spritz" hot kids with cool water.

3. We will need one parent to tally the pledge sheets so they go home with the students that day.

4. We will need two parents to stand at your classroom's refreshment table and distribute refreshments.

We will have a brief parents' meeting on the morning of the Walkathon (Tuesday, November 1) fifteen minutes prior to each work shift.

The shifts will be as follows:

      A.M. KINDERGARTEN—10:45 A.M.
      P.M. KINDERGARTEN & GRADES 1–3—12:45 P.M.
      GRADES 4–6—1:45 P.M.

Each shift will last approximately an hour and a half.

If you have any questions, you may call either _____ or _____ .

                    Sincerely,
                    The Walkathon Committee

Dear Teachers:

The PTA wishes to express our thanks to all of you for all the support, cooperation, and help you have given us for our Walkathon. We never could have done it without you.

Attached you will find the pledge sheets and cover letters for all the walkers who have monies to be collected. Please send these home today. The children are to return all money and pledge sheets by _____ . Please send these to _____ as they come in.

Thank you again for your support.

                                     The Walkathon Committee

To the Parents and Walkathon Sponsors of _____ :

Attached you will find your Walkathon pledge sheet with the number of laps completed and the total to be collected filled in. The total to be collected has been either written in red or circled in red. After the money is collected, indicate the amount collected in the "Total Collected" column. It is now up to the walkers to collect their pledges.

All monies must be returned to school WITH YOUR PLEDGE SHEET by _____ . Please put money and pledge sheet in an envelope marked with the child's name and homeroom teacher. Cash or checks are acceptable. Please make checks payable to the Lincoln School PTA.

Once again, thank you all for your support in making the Walkathon a success.

                                     The Walkathon Committee

Dear Teacher:

Attached you will find three Walkathon envelopes with your name on each of them. Please use these envelopes for collected Walkathon money. Use one per day, every day that money comes in. These envelopes will be returned to you for reuse.

Please send the envelopes to _____ 's office daily.

Thank you,
The Walkathon Committee

Walkathon Reminder to Students

Please don't forget to turn in your pledge sheet with your Walkathon money. All money is due by _____ .

Thank you,
The Walkathon Committee

Dear Students, Parents, and Walkathon Sponsors:

Our Second Annual Walkathon was another great success. We would like to thank all those who participated in this event. The children were wonderfully enthusiastic and encouraged each other on to walk additional laps. The teachers gave total cooperation to this project, and we couldn't have done it without their help. Our principal, _____ , gets a big thank-you for coordinating all the classes to start and stop on time. A special thanks also goes to all the parents who helped out during the Walkathon. And we can't forget all the sponsors, who were exceedingly generous in their donations. Thank you, one and all.

We are very pleased to announce that the Walkathon has collected just over $4,500 to date. This money will be used to enhance the educational experience of our students in various ways.

A number of pledges have not come in yet. Please turn them in as soon as possible.

At the last PTA meeting, approval was given to the following spending requests:

1. Purchase of a VCR for the library.
2. Purchase of a number of library books requested by the library.
3. Purchase of materials for a "Big Book" project for the kindergartens.
4. $50.00 for each classroom teacher for the children to determine what the class would like to purchase for their efforts.
5. $500.00 to be added to the existing Lincoln School Scholarship fund for Lincoln students in need of financial assistance.

Other spending requests that were tabled for the fall were purchase of carpeting for the kindergarten classes and purchase of a copy machine for the school.

Again, we would like to thank all of you for making our Walkathon the huge success that it was. We are looking forward to doing it again next year.

Sincerely,
The Walkathon Committee

CHAPTER TWO

ACADEMIC MARATHONS: KNOWLEDGE-A-THONS, READATHONS, MATHATHONS, AND SPELLATHONS

I<small>F A WALKATHON IS EASY, AN ACADEMIC MARATHON IS EVEN</small> easier—you don't even have to set up the track, count the laps the children walk, or serve juice. At the same time, you're encouraging the children to learn!

Last year, an elementary school hosted a spellathon; teachers gave their pupils spelling tests, and donors pledged a certain amount for each correct answer. This year the school is planning to have a mathathon, doing the same thing with math tests prepared by the teachers at each grade level.

"Once you get a mathathon or spellathon going, and it's well organized, very often it can provide all of the funding you need for one year and eliminate the need for a half-dozen other fund-raisers, which drive the parents crazy!" says Barb Daugherty, a PTA president in Redlands, California.

KNOWLEDGE-A-THON

A Pennsylvania elementary school hosts a knowledge-a-thon every year. Children at each grade level are given 100 age-appropriate facts and two months to learn them, after which they're quizzed by a teacher or parent. They ask sponsors to pledge to donate so much for each fact learned or to make a flat donation. Students are rewarded with T-shirts, sports bags, sweatshirts, or backpacks, depending on the amount of money they collect from sponsors. Those getting all 100 questions correct have their names displayed on a plaque at school and are invited to a dinner prepared by teachers and staff.

See the forms following p. 26 for samples of the facts that first- and fifth-graders were asked to learn one year, the pledge sheet that the school uses, and instructions given to the parent volunteers who test the children.

READATHON

A readathon raises as much as $5,000 per year at an eleven hundred student magnet school in St. Paul, Minnesota. The readathon is successful not only in raising funds for the school library and reading program but also in generating enthusiasm for reading. Students get sponsors who pledge to pay a specified amount for each book (or chapter of a book) that the students read or have read to them in February.

The month of February revolves around reading. The PTO hosts its book fair late in the month. All sorts of people are invited to come to the school and read to the children: parents, grandparents, local politicians, school board members, authors, and school personnel not usually seen reading (janitors, secretaries, cafeteria workers, and the principal). In the examples following p. 26 you'll find copies of the invitations sent to family members and others asking them to come in and read aloud.

The school has a diverse student body—40 percent minority—drawn from all over St. Paul. Middle-income parents sponsor those students who don't have other sponsors so that all children can participate. Because February is Black History Month, books by black authors or about black history count double.

The classes that read the most books get prizes—popcorn parties or plaques and money. Each student who participates gets a bookmark, and the student in each grade who reads the most gets $5 worth of tickets for the spring carnival.

The first year the school hosted a readathon, 70 percent of classes participated, and they raised $3,000. The second year, 80 percent of classes helped to earn $4,000, and the third year, all classes participated, and they raised $5,000. The only expenses each year are $20 for plaques for the two classes that read the most books, between $200 and $300 for printing, and the cost of forty bags of popcorn!

A letter sent home to parents with information on the readathon appears among the samples that follow this page. In addition, the PTO sent out suggested reading lists.

PLANNING AND PREPARATION

Planning and preparing for an academic marathon is simple and straightforward. Refer to "Step-by-Step Planning and Preparation" in Chapter 1 (pp. 7–12) and the letters and forms following this page, and you're all set to begin!

———✳——✳——✳———

First-Grade Knowledge-a-thon

1. What three colors appear on the American flag? RED, WHITE, BLUE

2. What was the name of astronaut Commander Thout's space flight? ATLANTIS

3. How many planets are in our solar system? NINE (9)

4. What is the name of the imaginary line that divides the earth into two equal parts between the North and the South? EQUATOR

5. Name the three main parts of a plant. ROOT, STEM, LEAVES

6. What name is given to the answer in an addition problem? SUM

7. What name is given to the answer in a subtraction problem? DIFFERENCE

8. Who invented the light bulb? THOMAS EDISON

9. Name two wind instruments. OBOE, CLARINET, SAXOPHONE, FLUTE, BASSOON

10. How many notes are in an octave? EIGHT (8)

11. Which president is pictured on a nickel? THOMAS JEFFERSON

12. What was John Chapman's nickname? JOHNNY APPLESEED

13. Name two (2) things that all living things need. WATER, AIR, LIGHT, FOOD

14. Name two (2) states that touch Pennsylvania. NEW YORK, OHIO, NEW JERSEY, DELAWARE, MARYLAND, WEST VIRGINIA

15. How many legs do spiders have? EIGHT (8)

16. How many body segments does an insect have? THREE (3)

17. Who was the first president to ride on a railroad train? ANDREW JACKSON

18. We have lungs. What does a fish have? GILLS

19. What is the name of our largest state? ALASKA

20. What famous inventor tied a key to the end of a kite? BENJAMIN FRANKLIN

21. What do you call a person who writes music? COMPOSER

22. What is a butterfly before it is a butterfly? CATERPILLAR

Fifth-Grade Knowledge-a-thon

1. Our nation's capital is located on the banks of this river. POTOMAC RIVER

2. What is the "City of Brotherly Love"? PHILADELPHIA

3. Name the original thirteen colonies. MASSACHUSETTS, RHODE ISLAND, NEW JERSEY, PENNSYLVANIA, CONNECTICUT, NEW YORK, DELAWARE, MARYLAND, VIRGINIA, NEW HAMPSHIRE, NORTH CAROLINA, SOUTH CAROLINA, and GEORGIA

4. Who wrote "The Star-Spangled Banner"? FRANCIS SCOTT KEY

5. Who was the only president from Pennsylvania? JAMES BUCHANAN

6. Who wrote the Declaration of Independence? THOMAS JEFFERSON

7. Name the three branches of the U.S. government. EXECUTIVE, LEGISLATIVE, JUDICIAL

8. Name the Great Lakes. ERIE, SUPERIOR, HURON, ONTARIO, MICHIGAN

9. What professional baseball player hit the most home runs? HANK AARON

10. Who invented the telephone? ALEXANDER GRAHAM BELL

11. Who was the first person to walk on the moon? NEIL ARMSTRONG

12. Where is the rainiest spot in the forty-eight contiguous states? MOUNT OLYMPUS IN THE STATE OF WASHINGTON

13. What devastating storm has a funnel-shaped cloud? TORNADO

14. What type of fencing ended the open range of the American West? BARBED WIRE

15. By what name are the northernmost native Americans known? ESKIMOS or INUITS

16. The geographic center of North America is located in which state? NORTH DAKOTA

17. The Suez Canal connects what two bodies of water? MEDITERRANEAN SEA and RED SEA

18. In which two hemispheres is the United States located? NORTHERN and WESTERN

19. What is the longest river in the world? NILE

Knowledge-a-thon Pledge Sheet

Sponsor's Name	Pledge Per Question	No. of Questions Answered	Total Donation
1.			
2.			
3.			
4.			
5.			
6.			
7.			
8.			
9.			
10.			
11.			
12.			
13.			
14.			
15.			
16.			
17.			
18.			
19.			
20.			

Student _____ Room _____

Total questions answered correctly _____

Total amount collected _____

Knowledge-a-thon Testing Guidelines

1. On memorization pieces, students may miss a word or two in selections and still be given credit.

2. Be flexible, not rigid, in accepting answers. E.g., Franklin for Ben Franklin.

3. Don't give clues or hints.

4. If student can't remember an answer, only go back and give the question again if the student has a chance of getting 100 out of 100.

5. Student will generally either know or not know the answer. Keep moving right along.

6. Record the names of the students you tested and turn them in to office. (This will help if any questions arise.)

7. Record student scores on the half-sheet and give it to student.

8. Thanks for your help. (If you have any suggestions for next year's testing, please let us know.)

Dear Mom, Dad, Relative, Guardian, or Friend:

WHAT: Will you please read aloud in my classroom?

WHERE: Room_____

WHY: We can all enjoy listening together, and our class can write on our Readathon sheets that you read *to* us and *with* us. The more reading we HEAR and DO in February, **the more $ we raise** for our school library and reading program. We also read for the fun of it.

WHEN: Throughout the month of February. The ideal time time for you to read in our homeroom is between_____ and_____ (time) on_____(day of the week). My teacher wants to know the best time for YOU!

HOW: Send my teacher,_____, a note, or phone_____ and leave a message telling her/him YOUR favorite time to read in class. Read for five minutes or longer. My teacher will let you know *when* and *how long* you get to read in our room.

READ! How about reading us a chapter?! a poem?! a comic strip, tongue-twister, joke, or limerick?! a bit of a book liked by you or your family?! We'll be positive listeners!

                Sincerely,

                _____

                Parent Teacher Organization (PTO)

P.S. You can read in my room even if I don't have "sponsors" or any books read. The Readathon is over at the end of February. ACT QUICKLY!

Dear Friends of Reading:

The Parent-Teacher Organization of _____ Elementary School is sponsoring a Readathon during the month of February. The purpose of the Readathon is twofold. First we would like to encourage our children to become more involved with books. We want them to be exposed to a wide variety of literature and print material. We would like them to experience both reading to themselves and being read to by others. The second purpose of the Readathon is to raise money for the school.

We would like to invite you to come to school as a guest reader. We have found that guest readers add to the excitement of the program. They also show our children that reading is important to everybody!

You can volunteer to read in one classroom for ten minutes, or you can volunteer to read in several classrooms. You can bring your favorite story, or we can provide you with some material. Please call _____ , the school librarian, at _____ . She will arrange a time for you to share some magical moments with our children.

Sincerely,
Parent-Teacher Organization (PTO)

P.S. If you know of anyone else who is interested in helping out, please pass a copy of this letter to him or her.

LINCOLN SCHOOL READATHON

Student_____ Teacher_____ Room_____

Dear Sponsor,

The Lincoln School Readathon will add books to our school library and reading program. It raises money and also encourages students to read! No. of Books = books, poetry, magazine and newspaper articles read or heard by students at home or at school. It's Black History Month, so any reading by black authors or related to black history or culture counts double. Thank you for your pledge per-title-read or your donation.

Parent Teacher Organization (PTO)

Name of Sponsor	Pledge or Contribution per Book		No. of Books Read	$ Owed	Date Collected
Examples					
Jane Doe	*50 cents*	*. . .*	*10*	*$5.00*	*March 1*
John Smith	*. . .*	*$4.00*	*. . .*	*$4.00*	*March 2*
1.	$	$		$	
2.	$	$		$	
3.	$	$		$	
4.	$	$		$	
5.	$	$		$	
6.	$	$		$	
7.	$	$		$	
8.	$	$		$	
9.	$	$		$	
10.	$	$		$	
11.	$	$		$	
12.	$	$		$	
13.	$	$		$	
14.	$	$		$	
15.	$	$		$	
16.	$	$		$	
17.	$	$		$	
18.	$	$		$	

Please make checks payable to LINCOLN SCHOOL PTO. (Prefer no cash, but will accept it.)

Books • Stories • Magazines • Newspapers • Poems I read, or were read to me.

Title	No. of Pages	Title	No. of Pages
1.		8.	
2.		9.	
3.		10.	
4.		11.	
5.		12	
6.		13.	
7.		14.	

Total Pages _____

Add another sheet if you get more sponsors or read more books.

. . . a reminder to read

Dear Parents and Guardians:

Please help our kids with sponsors and with reading by the end of February!

- Help get sponsors or contributions of money. Check at work, with friends, etc. If parents focus on the fund-raising, students can focus on the fun of reading.
- Encourage reading at home every spare minute through the end of February!
- Encourage writing down the pages and titles read (or heard).
- Schedule a time and read aloud for ten minutes in your child's classroom.
- February is Black History month, so books by black authors or about black history **count double!**

P.S. When you're at conferences in February, visit the **Book Fair** near the cafeteria. Excellent multicultural books will be available this year! PTO's major fund-raisers are the Book Fair, Spring Fling, and Readathon. Your support of these three events is appreciated. **Read aloud to each other, read silently, read side-by-side, R E A D !**

Parent-Teacher Organization (PTO)

CHAPTER THREE

BOOK FAIRS

Imagine an event that raises thousands of dollars, gives parents and children the opportunity to enjoy books together, and shows kids that reading can really be fun! Organizing a super book fair takes a lot of work, but it can pay off in more ways than one. Follow the guidelines in this chapter and your book fair is sure to be an event the whole school will look forward to, year after year.

CHOOSING A BOOK SUPPLIER: SHOULD YOU WORK WITH A BIG COMPANY OR A SMALLER ONE?

Several large companies are in the exclusive business of doing book fairs. (See the list on p. 51.) There are quite a few advantages to working with a large company, and if this is your first experience running a book fair, it is the simplest way to get started.

You'll make a high profit margin

The company will do a lot of the work for you

The company will send you posters and "how-to" information (at least one company even sends an instruction video)

Typically, when you work with one of these companies, your school retains cash profit of a percentage of sales revenue, ranging from 30 to 50 percent, depending on volume. In addition, the school keeps a certain dollar amount of the unsold stock at the end of the book fair, and it earns bonus points that can be redeemed for books and equipment. There is often room to negotiate the percentage of cash profit or the number of free books.

The large companies make life easy for you by delivering the books on rolling bookcases, color coded by appropriate age group. All you have to do is open up the bookcases and start selling. They select the books for you, and you don't even have to do an inventory.

The downside of working with big companies is that you can't select the titles you want. If they offer hardcover titles, the selection is usually quite limited. Often the selection of paperback books includes some classics, such as *Charlotte's Web*, along with a heavy dose of popular titles, such as the "Baby-sitters' Club" series and Nintendo strategy guides.

The Pros and Cons of Smaller Companies

If you want to offer a nice selection of hardcover books; books on parenting; foreign-language, science, or holiday books; books on any particular specialty topic or reading list; or computer software, you'll want to work with a smaller company or perhaps a local bookstore. They'll be willing to cater to your needs but will give you a smaller profit margin, usually around 20 percent of your revenue. The smaller companies deliver or have you pick up books in boxes, which you then display on tables.

When selecting a small company, find out whether it requires you to purchase books outright or whether it will let you sell on consignment and return what doesn't sell. Find out whether the company allows you to reorder books and how long it would take to get them.

Some schools decide to hold their book fair at a local bookstore. Parents are asked to shop at the store during one day or evening. (Sometimes the store is closed to the public during this time.) The school gets to keep 10 or 20 percent of the proceeds of any purchases that parents make then.

MULTIPLE SUPPLIERS

If you want the best of both worlds and don't mind doing a lot of extra bookkeeping, you can deal with multiple suppliers. Some of the smaller companies do beginning and ending inventories for you, and bill you for what you've sold, less the share you get to keep. Some small companies require the PTA to take inventories. The largest companies do not require you to inventory their books but simply to keep track of the dollar amount of your sales. This procedure is straightforward if you are selling only their books but can otherwise become complicated. (Detailed information on keeping track with multiple suppliers is provided on pp. 51–52.)

TIMING AND SCHEDULING

What's the Best Time of Year?

The most profitable book fairs are held in late fall, timed to coincide with other activities that draw parents to the school. Holding your book fair in November and offering both hardcover and softcover titles can double your potential profit, since you're giving parents the chance to buy great books as holiday gifts.

National Children's Book Week is in mid-November. Many schools schedule their book fairs then, sometimes in conjunction with a visit from an author of children's books.

Some schools hold book fairs in the spring, often as a second fair. This timing presents an excellent opportunity for teachers to draw up summer reading lists of books that are then stocked at the book fair.

Should You Hold an Off-Season Book Fair?

Some book fair companies offer inducements to hold book fairs in the winter or very early fall. Typically they might offer an extra 5 percent of revenue for off-season book fairs. That sounds attractive until you realize that parents will not buy many books in January, nor do they give their children much money to spend at that time of year. Your profit will be much higher in November than January as long as you sell at least 5 percent more books, as you most surely will.

Hours of Operation

If you choose to have your book fair during the week, plan to have it open half an hour before school opens and close half an hour after school lets out. Parents who drop off and pick up their children will stop by then, and a surprising number of children will need to shop at those times, even if their classes visited the fair during normal school hours. (Some children who were absent or forgot to bring their money when their classes visited the fair will come on their own later in the week.)

In addition, it's essential to be open at least one evening for the convenience of working parents. If staffing the fair during the entire school day proves difficult, you can close for an hour or two at lunchtime.

Getting the Kids There

Most schools schedule their book fairs during the week and bring classes of students through twice—a first trip to draw up wish lists to take home to Mom and Dad for approval, and then a return trip to make the actual purchases.

Other schools bring each class through just once. They send home an order form prior to the book fair, with the children then visiting the fair to make purchases from their lists, or they ask that children bring a small amount of money to school ($3 or $5) on a certain day and allow them to make their own selections.

Of course, either of these approaches takes time away from classroom study and can hurt those students who don't have money to buy books. Most schools justify the practice by arguing that a visit to a book fair can foster an interest in reading, that the time involved is minimal, and that the funds go to a good cause.

In one school, the PTA appropriates funds to the school social worker so that she can give $5 in spending money to each of the poorest children. A New Jersey school distributes a pack of four books to each teacher to be given out as she sees fit. Another school instructs teachers to identify and escort these children through the book fair, again at PTA expense. Susie Blecker, chairwoman of a New York book fair, says, "It made me feel wonderful to see these children's faces light up as they made their selections."

If you decide against having children visit the book fair during school hours, you can still hold your book fair during the week, making sure to have extensive after-school hours, or you can conduct your fair over the weekend. Local authors are sometimes willing to visit a weekend book fair to autograph their books.

Getting the Parents There

Most parents will not pay a special visit to a school book fair but will stop by if they happen to be at school for another reason. (By the way, your best customers will be your parent volunteers!) You can plan your book fair to coincide with a holiday concert, parent-teacher conference, Election Day, or an evening program or spaghetti dinner. If you sponsor an evening program or dinner, keep the book fair open for an hour or so afterward.

THEMES AND CONTESTS

You might consider a theme for the book fair. One school chose as its theme "Reading Is Magic," the title of the show performed by a magician on family night. Decorating according to this theme is easy, and you could sponsor a reading contest around it. For the month before the book fair, each time a child read a book, he or she would complete an entry form and drop it into a black hat in the school's lobby. During the fair, someone could pull ten names from the hat, with each winner receiving a $5 gift certificate to the book fair. You can sponsor a poster contest if you'd like. Prizes can be $5 gift certificates to the book fair. (These really cost you less than $5 each out of pocket.)

BOOK FAIR BONUSES

Even Better Than an Apple—the Teacher Registry

If your school permits giving gifts to teachers (check with the administration first), you can set up a "Teacher Registry"—which works like a bridal registry. Ask each teacher to preview the book fair and fill out a form listing the books he would like to add to his classroom library corner. Parents then consult the lists and select books to give at holiday time or, in the case of a spring book fair, at the end of the year. As parents purchase books, they simply cross those titles from the lists.

Most teachers are delighted with these gifts, and parents appreciate being spared some difficult shopping!

Selection of Additional Books

When working with the largest book fair companies, at the conclusion of the fair you are entitled to select and keep some of the unsold books, typically equivalent to 20 percent of the dollar amount of books that you sold (usually up to a maximum dollar amount). Some schools choose to take all their profit in books, forgoing any cash profit. Making these selections can be a mammoth undertaking, and it needs to be done just when you're exhausted and facing the job of cleaning up after the book fair. So it pays to formulate a plan in advance.

You can delegate the entire task to the school librarian or reading specialist, although since the books are generally paperbacks they might not be best suited for the library. Alternatively, you can distribute the books among all the classrooms, perhaps giving new teachers the most. Ask the teachers for guidance by having them draw up lists of books that they'd like.

Gifts to the School Library

You might also set up a system whereby parents can donate books to the school library. Have your librarian draw up a wish list. When parents visit the book fair and purchase books for the library, cross those titles from the list. Mark these books with bookplates containing the name of the donor, using the child's name: "This book has been donated to the library by Jennifer Smith." When Jennifer goes to the school library, she'll be able to look up the book and see her name in print!

PILFERAGE

When you return the unsold inventory to the company, it is your responsibility to pay for any missing books. That means that any lost books eat into your profit. But lost books are not necessarily stolen on purpose. As one New Jersey book fair chair says: "Kids walk off with things because they want to have them and may not realize that they must be paid for. This may be the first independent shopping experience for some of these kids."

A few simple precautions can guard against losses. The rolling bookcases can generally be locked after hours. Make sure that everything else is in a room that can be locked. You can use old sheets to cover items on tables. During the fair, position the cashiers at the door. You can stamp and bag each book that's been paid for, and ask children who've made their purchases to stand in a group at the door.

STEP-BY-STEP PLANNING AND PREPARATION

Stage One (Six Months Before)

THE COMMITTEE

The chair of the book fair, herself nominated by the person in charge of fund-raising for the PTA, should form the book fair committee by finding volunteers to fill the following positions:

> liaison with school personnel
> liaison with book supplier(s)
> finance chair
> volunteer coordinator
> evening program chair

publicity chair

chair of setup, cleanup, and decorations

Hold a preliminary meeting of the committee to spell out responsibilities and make overall organizational decisions, such as when and where (gym, cafeteria, auditorium, or library) to have the book fair, what supplier(s) to use, what hours to operate the book fair, whether to have a theme and/or contest as part of the book fair (and if so, what it will be), and what performer to use for the evening program if you choose to have one.

Liaison with School Personnel

Clear the chosen place and dates with your school principal and librarian.

Liaison with Book Supplier(s)

Book the supplier(s). Negotiate dates and terms.

Evening Program Chair

Talk to PTA members at nearby schools to get names of performers, and preview performers if the district PTA hosts a preview day. Book the performer, and ask him or her for any brochures or posters that you could use for publicity.

Stage Two (One to Four Weeks Before)

Have another meeting of the entire committee about a month before the fair to bring everyone up to date and to work out any problems that may have arisen. At this point each chair should do the following:

Liaison with School Personnel

Meet with the principal and/or custodial staff to:

reiterate dates and place

request custodial help and equipment (tables, chairs, microphones, adding machines, showcase or bulletin board space)

Touch base with the librarian to coordinate efforts. Ask the librarian or art teacher to have students make posters publicizing the upcoming book fair. If you'll be having a poster contest, start it now.

About two weeks before the book fair, send a memo to teachers to let them know that the fair is coming up, and ask them to choose time slots for their classes. A sample letter appears at the end of the chapter. (In some schools, the principal does the scheduling.) Ask teachers not to hand out book orders for the few weeks prior to the book fair. Often books sold at the book fair are less expensive when purchased through book orders, and parents become irritated at paying more at the book fair. Post sign-up sheets on a bulletin board or in the main office. If you plan to have two classes visiting the book fair at a time, you might want to indicate on the sign-up sheets that there be one class of younger children and one of older children in each time slot. About a week before the fair, check the sign-up sheets to make sure that all teachers are accounted for. Make a copy of the schedule, and keep one copy in the office and the other at the book fair (so the volunteer coordinator can check off classes as they arrive).

Liaison with Book Supplier(s)

About a month before the fair, reconfirm arrangements as to dates, terms, and delivery of books. Select books if working with a small company.

Finance Chair

Decide how many cashboxes you'll use at the fair. You should have at least one person taking money for each class touring the fair at a given time. For instance, if two classes of twenty-five students will be making purchases together, you should have at least two volunteers taking money. If you expect a big crowd at family night, you could have three tables set up with two cashboxes at each table.

Make sure you know how to make deposits at the bank, and get the necessary deposit slips and the signature stamp for depositing checks. Alert the PTA treasurer that she'll need to write a check to the supplier after the book fair.

If you plan to allow students to order books that have sold out, formulate a plan to do so. Require that all orders be prepaid, and make sure that you have receipts to give people who've placed orders, as well as a master form on which you'll note orders for your own records. (You should buy receipts with carbons or duplicate forms at an office supply store. That way, you'll have a copy of the receipts you've given students and thus be able to check the individual orders against your master form.) On your form, you'll need to list the student's name, phone number, teacher, and what's been ordered. You'll also need brightly colored removable stickers to put on the last copy of each title, so that when someone tries to buy one of these books you'll know that it's the last and that you need to take an order for it rather than sell it.

Checklist for supplies:

metal cashbox with lock

start-up change of at least $30 in one-dollar bills and rolls of change

printing calculator or adding machine

bags

sales tax chart if needed

garbage can

paper clips

scrap paper

rubber bands, stapler, and tape

decorative stamp to mark books as paid

brightly colored stickers to put on last copy of each title if you allow reorders

receipts for back orders

master reorder form

thirty sharpened pencils and pencil holder

PUBLICITY CHAIR

Send a note home to parents to announce the book fair. Give dates, and ask for volunteers to work during the fair. The volunteer coordinator and you can compose the memo together so that it includes a calendar of available time slots. Parents can simply fill in their names in the preferred time slots and return their forms to the PTA mailbox. Schools that schedule the time slots for classes early are able to let parents know when their children will be visiting the fair so parents can volunteer to be there when their own children are shopping.

Write a press release (a sample is provided at the end of the chapter), and mail it to local newspapers two weeks prior to the book fair. (Check with your principal first, since school policy sometimes prohibits inviting outsiders to school.)

VOLUNTEER COORDINATOR

Go through whatever lists of volunteers you've accumulated through PTA meetings and other sign-up sheets. Make telephone calls to arrange the schedule, and fill in slots as needed. If two classes are going to visit the fair at a time, you'll need about six volunteers per shift, so schedule eight in case one or two can't make it at the last minute. Make sure that one person from the book fair committee is at the fair at all times; appoint someone in charge of each morning and afternoon of operation. It's exhausting for the book fair chair to be present every hour the fair is open.

Draft a letter to the volunteers to be sent home a week before the book fair. Start out by reconfirming their time slots: "Thank you for volunteering to work at the book fair. We have you scheduled to work on _____ from _____ to _____ . If you cannot make this time, please call _____ ." Include instructions on the volunteers' duties at the fair.

EVENING PROGRAM CHAIR

Finalize arrangements with the performer, asking what equipment she'll need and sending her directions to the school.

CHAIR OF SETUP, CLEANUP, AND DECORATIONS

Let the volunteer coordinator know how many people will be needed to help set up and clean up. Decide on a plan for what to do with children if the work will need to be done before or after school. You can hire baby-sitters, assign a parent the responsibility of supervising the children, or simply ask that parents make other arrangements for them. You'll also need a big sign or banner to post outside the school. If you have a display case in the school entry hall, line up someone artistic to decorate it about a week beforehand. Plan any extra decorations—balloons, banners, flowers—that you will need for the room in which the book fair will be held, and line up a decorating crew.

Make the teacher registry book if you plan to have one. Go to a local toy store or children's bookstore, and ask for a donation of bags (one for each student).

Checklist of supplies:

supplies for finance chair (see pp. 43 and 44)

school's supplies (see p. 44)

volunteer name tags

volunteer and teacher schedules

balloons and other decorations

Stage Three (the Day Before)

LIAISON WITH SCHOOL PERSONNEL

Send teachers a second memo, reminding them of the times that they've signed up to visit the fair and informing them of the procedures to follow. (Be sure each child brings a pencil. Ask teachers to register at the teacher registry, if you plan to have one.)

LIAISON WITH BOOK SUPPLIER(S)

Pick up the books if you have to, and inventory them if necessary. If anything is missing, contact the supplier immediately. The largest companies can usually deliver on a daily basis. One year a school working with a large company got its books delivered on the Friday before the book fair. A volunteer noticed that one of the rolling bookcases the school was supposed to get wasn't delivered. She called the company, and the missing case was at the school at 7:00 A.M. on Monday morning.

You might decide that you don't want to sell some of the merchandise that the company ships—books with sexually mature themes or those concerning topics such as suicide; merchandise of inferior quality; videotapes; or posters. In that case, simply keep that merchandise in boxes and don't display it.

PUBLICITY CHAIR

If children are going to visit the fair with their classes one time only, send a memo home with them the day before the book fair. Invite parents to visit the fair, and ask them to send in a nominal sum for their children to be able to spend themselves. If you're working with a large company, you'll have newspapers for each child listing all the titles for sale. Send those home with the memo.

VOLUNTEER COORDINATOR

Make reminder telephone calls to each volunteer the night before she's scheduled to work.

CHAIR OF SETUP, CLEANUP, AND DECORATIONS

As you set up the book fair, organize it so that books for each age group are kept together. Position the checkout close to the door, and keep all little items, such as pencils, erasers, and bookmarks, at the cash registers. If you plan to allow reorders when books sell out, put the bright, peel-off stickers on the last copy of each title. Place the sticker by the price so that the cashier will see it and won't sell that one but will know to take an order for it. When you're finished setting up, make sure to lock the room.

Stage Four (the Day of the Fair)

The volunteer coordinator should put some volunteers on the floor (to assist the children and keep things tidy) and some on checkout (to take money, bag books, and fill out reorder forms and receipts). Appoint one volunteer to greet shoppers and volunteers at the door.

Keep the schedule of volunteers handy, and check off names as people arrive for work, so you can thank them later. Have name tags on hand for the volunteers. You can even go so far as to have the book fair chairs adorned with hats or bandannas.

Also keep the schedule of classes close by, and check off classes as they arrive. If a class is very late, investigate.

If the children are to visit the fair twice, once to preview and once to purchase, be sure that on their first visit their teachers distribute the newspapers listing all the books for sale. Have the children record their choices on these papers or on a separate sheet. Ask teachers to send each child home with a letter from the PTA saying that the child visited the book fair, stating his choices and how to pay, and asking parents to indicate what they'd like their child to purchase. (See sample letter at the end of the chapter.)

When the kindergartners come in, have them wait at the door and have volunteers escort them two by two through the book fair. (Assuming you have enough volunteers, this system takes less time than having all kindergartners browsing aimlessly at once.)

After children have paid, put their books in bags and have them wait near the door.

If the book fair is going to be open following an evening performance, have lots of check-out lines and lots of people on the floor to answer questions. Having the book fair in a large area such as a gym is ideal if it will be open after an evening performance.

The finance chair should make daily bank deposits, and secure the cashboxes and books after hours. If you're working with a large company, you can probably reorder books every day, and, if you call early enough, you might even have the books the next day. The liaison with the company should do the reordering. If you notice that a title is very popular, ask for additional copies on the first day of the fair.

Stage Five (the Day After)

LIAISON WITH BOOK SUPPLIER(S)

Call in your last reorder.

FINANCE CHAIR

Calculate total receipts, and write the checks to the suppliers.

CHAIR OF SETUP, CLEANUP, AND DECORATIONS

Do an ending inventory if necessary. If you are able to keep some of the unsold stock, make your selections (see "Selection of Additional Books" on p. 40). The school librarian and/or several people from the clean-up squad should work on this time-consuming task. First, the finance chair needs to calculate the total dollar amount of free books to which the school is entitled and divide by the number of teachers to get a per-teacher allotment, maybe giving new teachers, the librarian, or the reading specialist an extra-large allotment. The clean-up crew should get grocery bags and label them with each teacher's name. Once the finance chair has figured a per-teacher dollar amount of books, the bags can be filled with books from each teacher's wish list on the teacher registry. Return unsold stock to the supplier.

Stage Six (One Week After)

LIAISON WITH SCHOOL PERSONNEL

Thank the custodial staff, librarian, and principal, and report on how much money was raised and how many free books you got. Send the teachers a memo doing the same.

LIAISON WITH BOOK SUPPLIER(S)

Call to discuss how the fair went. Distribute reorders to students by bagging them or putting rubber bands around each order, enclosing your copy of the individual reorder receipt. Put the children's names on their bags, and distribute all orders to the classroom teachers at the same time, if you can.

FINANCE CHAIR

Submit a financial report to the PTA president.

PUBLICITY CHAIR

In the next PTA newsletter, mention how successful the book fair was and thank parents for their support.

VOLUNTEER COORDINATOR

Send thank-you notes to all the volunteers, inviting them to a thank-you tea or breakfast.

Stage Seven (One Month After)

Call a meeting of the entire committee to discuss how things went—what worked and what you'd do differently next time. You can go out to lunch or have a tea at the chair's house. Ask each subcommittee chair to come to the meeting with a report explaining what she did so that the job of the chairs will be easier next year.

BOOK FAIR COMPANIES

AKJ Book Fair
5609-2A Fisher's Lane
Rockville, Maryland 20852
1-800-922-6066

Chinaberry Book Service (extensive collection of fine
literature—sends catalogs to distribute to each child, and takes
orders rather than sending books to display)
2780 Via Orange Way, Suite B
Spring Valley, California 91978
1-800-776-2242

Scholastic Great American Book Fairs
330 Westport Avenue
Norwalk, Connecticut 06851
1-800-327-1894 or 1-800-272-2665

School Book Fairs
10100 SBF Drive
Pinellas Park, Florida 34666
1-800-347-3080

Troll Book Fairs
100 Corporate Drive
Mahwah, New Jersey 07430
1-800-446-3194

DEALING WITH MULTIPLE SUPPLIERS

Dealing with multiple suppliers enables you to offer a nice
selection of merchandise but requires some extra bookkeeping.
There are basically two approaches to take: Have people pay for
the merchandise at separate cashiers so that the money due the
different suppliers is kept separate, or have one cashier set up
but keep a log of sales from the suppliers other than the main
one.

   Either way, you must devise a plan for identifying merchandise from the different suppliers, unless you physically separate the merchandise and have cashiers in each location. The easiest way to differentiate the merchandise is by putting color-coded, removable stickers on each item that doesn't come from the main supplier.

For instance, if you're using a big company for most of your books, don't affix stickers to these books but put a bright yellow *removable* sticker next to the price on each item that comes from the local bookstore. At checkout, have several pieces of paper ready for volunteers to record the dollar amounts of sales of items with yellow stickers. Label the paper "SALES FROM the local bookstore," and put several of the bright yellow stickers at the top of the page for emphasis.

At the end of the fair, total the amounts on the sheets, and add up all the money that you took in. The difference between the dollar amount of all sales and the total on the sheets is the amount that you sold from the big company. If you're selling cookbooks, raffle tickets, or T-shirts at the same time, you can either take money separately for them or use another sheet to record those sales.

Whatever the system, don't make it too complicated for the volunteers. Over the course of the book fair, you'll have many different people taking money under sometimes hectic circumstances. Be sure to send instructions to the volunteers in advance explaining your system.

Carefully peel off all stickers before returning the books to the bookstore.

To: Lincoln Faculty

From: Book Fair Cochairs

Subject: The Book Fair

As cochairs of the book fair again this year, we wanted to let you know that the fair will be the week of November 1–5. We'll be selling paperback books from _____ and a big selection of books from _____ . We'll be open from 8:30 A.M. to 3:00 P.M. on Monday, Tuesday, Thursday and Friday; and on Tuesday evening, we'll reopen at 6:30 and close at 9:00 P.M.

_____ , along with several of his musician friends and the fifth- and sixth-grade chorus, will perform for family night on _____ at 7:00 P.M. in the gym. Their show, "Families," is free, and we invite you to attend.

The "teacher registry" was a big success last year, and we'll be having it again this year, both as a service to parents wanting to purchase holiday gifts and for use by the book fair committee. We're entitled to select hundreds of dollars of free books at the end of the fair, and the lists of what you could use help us very much in making those selections. We do the best we can to fill your lists based on what we have left in inventory at the end of the sale. Please stop by the book fair some time on _____ , to make a list of books you would like.

We'll have sign-up sheets posted in the front office on _____ . Please stop by and sign up your class to visit the book fair twice: once to preview and once to purchase. When your class comes to preview, we'll give each child a form on which to record his or her preferences, and we'll give you letters for each child to take home that night. Please have the children bring their own pencils to the book fair on preview day.

The entire book fair committee joins us in thanking you for your continued help. If you have any questions, please feel free to call either one of us.

Press Release

Dates: November 1–5

Subject: Book Fair at Lincoln School

Contact: Book Fair Cochair (at _____)

"Reading Is Magic" is the theme of Lincoln School's book fair this year, running November 1–5, from 8:30 A.M. to 3:00 P.M. A big selection of hardcover and paperback books and cassette tapes will be for sale, in time for holiday gift buying for children from kindergarten through junior high. The entire community is invited to visit the fair.

Magician _____ will perform on _____ at 7:00 P.M. in the gym. His show, _____ , promises to be highly entertaining. That evening, the book fair will be open from 6:30 to 9:00 P.M., and winners of the PTA raffle will be drawn.

Raffle prizes include _____ . In addition, ten children attending the performance will win door prizes of $5 gift certificates for _____ . Raffle tickets cost $1 each or six for $5, and they can be purchased at the book fair.

Book Fair—November 1–5

Dear Parents:

Children's Shopping: Your child visited the book fair today and drew up a wish list of books, which you should have, along with a newspaper printout of many of the books for sale. Please review the list and select which, if any, books you'd like to purchase, mark the items appropriately, and send in cash or a check for the total amount made payable to the Lincoln PTA. Classes will revisit the fair on another day to make actual purchases.

Your Shopping: We have a wonderful selection of gift books and cassettes this year in addition to the items in the newspaper handout. Please stop by personally to do some of your holiday shopping. You can shop on family night or before, during, or after school or parent-teacher conferences.

The school gets to keep 40 percent of what you spend on books from _____ and 20 percent of the others. In addition, at the end of the fair, we get to select from the unsold inventory free books totaling 20 percent of our _____ sales. We distribute the free books to the classroom teachers and library.

Hours: 8:30 A.M. – 3:00 P.M.   Monday, Tuesday, Thursday, and Friday
        6:30 P.M. – 9:00 P.M.   Tuesday for family night

Teacher Registry: Each teacher will preview the book fair, making a list of books that he or she would like. You can thus purchase a book and save it to give as a gift to your child's teacher, knowing that it's something desired. Over the past two years, teachers have been building terrific in-class libraries this way.

Gifts to Library: The librarian is also drawing up a wish list. When you purchase a book for the library, she'll affix a book plate stating "This book was donated to the Lincoln School Library by your child." She can arrange for you to donate a book in honor of your child's birthday.

Family Night: Bring your children to "Families," the musical performance that will take place in the gym tomorrow evening, _____ , at 7:00 P.M. Admission is free, and the book fair will be open both before and after the show. _____ and the fifth- and sixth-grade chorus will perform a medley of songs about families.

Volunteers: Many thanks to everyone who's volunteered to work at the book fair. If you haven't yet signed up to volunteer but would like to, please call _____ .

Book Fair Cochairs

CHAPTER FOUR

CLOTHESLINE SALES

ONE SCHOOL IN KANSAS CITY RAISES NEARLY $100,000 EACH year with a clothesline sale! Parents of the 1,000 students at the school donate much more than just clothing—books, furniture, baby equipment, electronics, tools, sporting goods, and you-name-it. For three days in April, two gyms and three tennis courts are transformed into a department store staffed by parent volunteers. Parents work a total of 11,500 hours. The 125 parents who are department chairs try to be present for the entire weekend of the sale.

The PTA of a 5,000-student school district near Rochester, New York, also has a huge clothesline sale every year, with more than 100 volunteers on duty each day for an entire week. At a recent sale, the PTA grossed $38,000 and, after paying expenses, netted about $23,000.

A full-fledged clothesline sale is thus a massive undertaking, probably the most difficult and time-consuming fundraiser. Those involved in clothesline sales think the effort pays off, though, in terms of both the amount of money they raise for their schools and the community service they provide—selling quality merchandise at affordable prices.

"It's a lot of work and a lot of fun," says Judy Hall, who cochaired the clothesline sale at the Kansas City school one year. "Through the clothesline sale you find camaraderie and make school friendships that can't be found anywhere else. It's a real close time for the entire school to be together, a sense of community. We hear what a need we're filling in the community. People wait every year for the clothesline sale to buy school clothes and furniture. We feel that we're doing a public service."

Even schools that have traditionally held large and successful clothesline sales are scaling back operations, however, because they face the problem of the "vanishing volunteer." For this reason, and because one chapter cannot provide enough detail for you to plan and organize a full-fledged clothesline sale, I instead describe a clothesline sale and go on to explain how to organize a more manageable sale of used sporting goods.

WHEN TO HAVE YOUR CLOTHESLINE SALE

Have your sale over a weekend in the fall or spring, at a time of year when people are moving, cleaning out closets, and shopping to buy things secondhand. Do some research to find out whether any other schools or charities are staging clothesline sales during the same season and coordinate dates so as not to compete on the identical weekend.

SHOULD YOU ACCEPT DONATIONS OF ALL SORTS?

If your school is having a sale for the first time, you might want to limit its scope—to used sporting goods, exercise equipment, baby equipment, toys, books, and dress shoes. Otherwise, you could feel overwhelmed with too much merchandise.

Even if you decide to have a full-fledged clothesline sale, you don't want to be left with a lot to dispose of at the end of the sale. Ask that people donate only "gently used items of good quality." Don't accept furniture so worn that it's unsalable or large appliances that you won't be able to donate to charity if they don't sell.

SHOULD YOU ALLOW GOODS TO BE SOLD ON CONSIGNMENT?

When schools sell goods on consignment, they share the proceeds of the sale with the owner in some prespecified way. The owner prices an item, and if it sells, the school keeps 25 percent and the owner 75 percent, or they split the proceeds fifty-fifty, for instance.

Schools that have large-scale clothesline sales generally do not take goods on consignment, because the bookkeeping would be too burdensome. They would have to keep track of how much each of thousands of items sold for and to whom the proceeds were due. As an additional complication, when goods are sold on consignment, owners must price each item or agree to the pricing set by the PTA. Prices cannot be marked down during the sale, unless the owners agree. When items' tags become lost, no one knows whose things they are and how they were priced, and often parents become angry if their goods are not accounted for at the end of the sale. In addition, when consignment goods are left unsold at the end of the sale, cleanup is complicated if donors are allowed to come in to claim their merchandise.

The school district near Rochester does accept items on consignment, sharing proceeds fifty-fifty with the consignees. Many people donate goods outright anyway. Dawn Gehrke says, "Some people like to donate knowing they're helping their neighbor or someone not as fortunate." Consignees must agree that most unsold merchandise will be donated to charity at the end of the sale. To alleviate the problems that occur when tags become separated from their items, consignees must describe their goods in detail on the tags and consignment sheets. Then if someone brings a tagless item to the cashier, a volunteer tries to match it with one of the tags found on the floor.

For smaller sales, taking goods on consignment is more manageable. Unquestionably, people donate more and nicer items when they are able to share in the sale proceeds, so it's simply a matter of weighing the additional donations against the added complications associated with consignments.

INVOLVING WORKING PARENTS, ALUMNI, AND THE ENTIRE COMMUNITY

Clothesline sales afford the perfect opportunity to involve working parents, alumni, and the entire community. Since the sales are usually held on weekends, most working parents are free to volunteer their time at least during the sale itself, and many of them enjoy this once-a-year commitment. Teachers and administrators volunteer their time, too.

The couple of days that the sale is actually running there's hard work to be done, but it's a lot of fun, too. Dads who don't like to volunteer for any other activity often enjoy volunteering at a clothesline sale—selling toys, clothes, electronics, or anything else for a day or two. After one dad telephoned many of them personally, 123 dads agreed to volunteer at one school's clothesline sale. Bonnie Pearson, volunteer coordinator of the Kansas City sale, comments that her school's clothesline sale "is probably the fastest means for new parents to get involved in the school."

Of course the sale's success hinges on the number of people in the community coming in to buy things. Some schools also invite residents and businesses in the community to donate items. Every year, one candy company accumulates gift wrap, ribbon, and store display items and sends about two trucks full of new merchandise to a local clothesline sale. Alumni (of private schools in particular) are also usually asked for donations. As a way of thanking donors, schools may invite them to shop at the sale before it opens to the public.

WHERE TO SET UP THE SALE

Schools provide the perfect setting for clothesline sales, because they generally have gyms and parking lots large enough to handle many cars.

Some schools set up everything indoors in gyms, cafeterias, and other large spaces. One school even uses its locker room as a dressing room. The Kansas City school uses two gyms and also erects a huge tent on the tennis courts, which are fenced in. (Obviously, security is a prime concern, because sales are set up for days at a time.) Furniture and other items that would be damaged by rain are put under cover of the tent, whereas bicycles, lawn furniture, swing sets, gas grills, and the like are set up outside (but within the tennis courts). One gym is devoted entirely to clothing, including a "designer's den" for very nice clothing. Everything else—electronics, books, toys, and collectibles—is in the other gym.

WHAT THE SALE IS LIKE

Shoppers generally line up for hours waiting for the doors to open—even in the rain. Once inside, they are asked to check bags and packages at the door. (Students sometimes work the bag-check area.) One school hands numbered tickets to shoppers awaiting entrance. Then the volunteers know whom to let in first and are able to restrict attendance to the limit allowed by the fire code.

Volunteers hand shoppers big clear plastic garbage bags to use while shopping. At one school, shopping carts and cardboard boxes are also available for shoppers.

The sale has been set up to look like a department store. Clothing is hung on racks, by size. Other items are displayed on tables or shelves. Volunteer department heads are stationed at each "department," wearing matching aprons, and other apron-clad volunteers walk the floor and are stationed at the doors. Unfortunately, shoplifting is sometimes a problem, so volunteers need to be on the lookout for it. At sales where goods are marked down right before closing, some shoppers stash merchandise early on, hoping to buy it at reduced prices. Volunteers try to make sure that items remain displayed where they belong.

Once a shopper has made her selections, she has to pay before leaving the gym. At the check-out area, there are separate lines for "ten items or less—cash only," cash only, checks, and, at most clothesline sales, MasterCard/Visa. Usually, two volunteers work at each station, one reading off prices and the other entering the figures into an adding machine or printing calculator. Students sometimes help by affixing "paid" stickers and bagging.

MasterCard and Visa

Call a few local banks to find out how to use MasterCard and Visa. It's not difficult to do, although you might choose not to accept credit cards if you decide that the amount charged (about

4 percent of sales) is not worth it or if you don't have access to telephone lines. You might even be able to find a bank that won't charge you a fee. You can still take credit cards even if you can't call to verify that the charger's credit is good and that the card isn't stolen. In that case, however, you take a loss if the company won't cover a charge.

HOURS OF OPERATION

Most clothesline sales run from late Thursday afternoon through Saturday. For the first day, the sales are usually closed to the public and open only to faculty and staff, donors, alumni, and either all parents or just those who volunteer at the sale. Volunteers can hand out admission tickets of different colors to people in the various categories, entitling them to enter at staggered times during "parent night." Roughly one-third of the $114,000 that one school grossed at its clothesline sale one year came from sales to faculty, staff, parents, and alumni the night before the sale opened to the public.

Sometimes sales are closed on Friday morning and open only after school's been dismissed at noon. Other schools open their doors at 9:00 A.M. on Friday, but only to donors or people who pay a small admission fee ($2 to $5). By Friday afternoon, most sales are fully open to the public.

On Saturday, schools start marking down their merchandise. Most often, everything is half price until noon. Then the sales close for half an hour to an hour while everything gets straightened up. When they reopen, for two hours or so they have a "bag-it sale." At the entrance, shoppers get bags, which they can fill for $5 each. One school uses plastic bags that are slightly larger than plastic grocery bags. It buys 1,000 of them for $40.

By midafternoon on Saturday, most sales have closed their doors. Charities have been invited to come at this time and take whatever they'd like from the unsold merchandise. Some schools invite just one charity each year, alternating charities from year to year, and others invite up to a dozen charities—ranging from Goodwill and the Salvation Army to shelters for battered women and the homeless. Judy Hall, of Kansas City, says that her school donated to a total of thirteen charities at the end of one sale, with the Salvation Army alone filling three trucks.

After the charities have taken what they want, whatever is left gets thrown out into Dumpsters that have been delivered a week or two before the sale. The Dumpsters have also been used during setup as donations have been sorted.

PUBLICITY

Once a clothesline sale becomes an annual event, people look forward to it and even defer purchases until they have a chance to attend. People sometimes travel from out of state—up to 100 miles away—to large sales, and long lines form outside for hours before opening time at nearly all of them.

Yet even with longtime clothesline sales, publicity committees work overtime to ensure success. They take out ads in local newspapers and try to get public service announcements on television and radio. One school advertises within a thirty-mile radius. Another takes out ads in the local "Penny Saver" (advertising newspaper), which draws from a large area. In addition, most schools try to get local newspapers to write human interest stories about their sales to generate publicity for them.

One school informed its cable TV community-access channel of its clothesline sale, and for two weeks the channel ran a videotape with footage of volunteers' setting up the sale and information about sale dates and times. Another even got a local theater chain to donate a screen slide in its advertising previews before movies. Volunteers post fliers all around town and huge signs and banners in front of the school. Most important, the publicity committees communicate well with parents, by telephoning and sending notices home. Parents and teachers at one school place signs on their cars advertising their sale a week or two ahead of time.

SHOULD YOU SELL FOOD?

Selling food at a clothesline sale makes a lot of sense. Shoppers are often hungry, having shopped for hours or traveled great distances to get there. In addition, you need to feed the volunteers who work long shifts.

Before arranging to sell food, check out local health ordinances and state law. New York State, for instance, doesn't allow any food other than cafeteria fare to be sold on public school property until the end of the last lunch period.

A school in Connecticut has always had a café, where volunteers sell soda, coffee, tea, premade and wrapped peanut-butter-and-jelly and turkey sandwiches, brownies, and cookies. One year local grocery stores donated hot dogs and rolls, and a parent set up a hot-dog truck in front of the school. The school made $1,000 selling hot dogs, cotton candy, and soda from the truck. The best customers were those waiting in line before the sale opened!

This particular school also sets up a gourmet table in the school entryway. Every single family is asked to donate something—brownies, a cake, a quiche, lasagna, pasta salad, cookies. Perishables are kept in the refrigerator and brought out during the course of the day. The school makes roughly $2,000 from the gourmet table, charging, for example, $10 for a pan of lasagna. Mary Jane Ackroyd, mother of two children at the school, says, "Every single family gets a call asking what they'll bring, and about a week before the sale they get a reminder postcard: 'Thank you for offering to bring _____ for the gourmet table at the clothesline sale. Please drop it off Friday morning in the _____ .' "

WHAT SORT OF EXPENSES WILL YOU INCUR?

Unlike some other fund-raisers, clothesline sales are expensive to run. One school incurs expenses of about $15,000 each year. Another's annual expenses are in the range of $1,000 to $1,500. Depending on what the school provides, you could have to pay for garbage removal, publicity, security guards, a maintenance crew, and rental of racks, tables, and other equipment. Naturally, you can expect to recoup your expenses and much more if your sale is well run, however.

DO YOU NEED TO GET GOVERNMENT PERMITS?

Check to see if your town or city requires you to get a permit for your clothesline sale. You'll definitely need a separate permit to serve food; check with your local health department early on to find out its requirements. In addition, you might be required by law to have a police officer on duty directing traffic. (Hire at least one additional security officer to patrol the grounds and to accompany the parent making bank deposits.)

THE BARE BONES OF GETTING READY FOR THE SALE

Receiving and Sorting Donated Goods

Schools that have maintenance crews at their disposal and adequate storage space begin collecting goods up to a year before their clothesline sales. Parents call throughout the year to say that they have furniture to donate. Someone from the furniture subcommittee might check out the furniture to make sure that it's in salable condition and then give the go-ahead to the maintenance crew for pickup.

Private schools with the very largest clothesline sales usually use eighteen-wheel, over-the-road trailers to store goods throughout the year. At one school, the maintenance department collects large items from three or four homes each week throughout the year, so that by January, five such trailers have been filled in anticipation of the April clothesline sale. (One trailer is full of supplies.) Also filled are 7,000 square feet of basement space in a building owned by a parent, who lets the school use the property free of charge.

Most schools also have "drop-off" or "blitz" days or nights well in advance of the sale, sometimes starting in the fall for a spring sale. At a school in Connecticut, beginning the first week in January, the receiving committee sets up some tables at the school and accepts donations for a few hours every

Thursday morning. In March, donations are received two mornings a week, and in April every morning for two weeks. When people bring items in, they're asked if they can stay for a moment to do their own sorting. A couple of volunteers are also on hand to sort. In addition, the school holds blitz nights in January, February, and March when about twenty people get together just to sort merchandise.

On blitz night the sorters examine each item carefully to make sure that it's only "gently used." Says Mary Jane Ackroyd: "Clothing that's stained or torn badly gets thrown away, and things that aren't too bad are given to charity. Everything that winds up at the sale is in very good shape. I buy clothes for my own children there every year." Volunteers look over toys and games carefully to make sure that they're in very good condition. Volunteers sort everything into huge cardboard boxes, one for each type of item—women's blouses, shoes, and so forth—and when a box is full its contents are transferred into black plastic bags, marked according to category, and stored. All clothing is put in one storage area, all furniture in another, and so forth. The school has secure storage rooms available expressly for this purpose.

At schools that don't have adequate facilities for storage, donations are usually accepted only during the week prior to the sale. Except for some donated items that are stored in the chairman's garage, the school district near Rochester begins accepting donations and consignments on Sunday for the sale that will open the following Thursday. It accepts donations Sunday afternoon, and Monday through Wednesday until 2:00 P.M. It encourages people to bring in clothing on hangers whenever possible.

Tagging and Pricing Donated Goods

Once the receiving crew has done its job, the pricing crew takes over. Most schools used to tag each item individually, but they've abandoned that practice. Pricing and tagging each individual item was the most time-consuming aspect of the entire sale. Moreover, one school found that when they used wire pinch price tags, customers would sometimes change price tags and, in doing so, would tear some of the clothing. Volunteers complained that their fingers hurt when they had to pinch the wire tags, and cashiers were confused when items came to them tagless. (Of course, if goods are being sold on consignment, they must be marked individually.)

Note that with the exception of good furniture, electronics, books, collectibles, housewares, and designer clothes, items need not be priced individually. One school, which displays clothing on racks and tables, does not use tags for most items. Huge signs listing prices are posted on the tables and on the wall above the racks. All belts might be fifty cents each, for instance, and all jeans $2 each. At the check-out table, there's a listing of prices for cashiers to refer to. The school still prices furniture and toys individually, using round white stickers as price tags. Toys are priced roughly at half retail price or less. (To get a sense of what retail price would be, consult the catalogs of catalog stores.)

You can tag items by color, using a gun tab (the type used in department stores) and tags from a wholesale supply house. Everything with a sticker of the same color is priced the same, and the price color codes are posted on huge signs on the walls. All blouses might be tagged blue, and the sign on the wall might indicate that all items marked with blue tags cost $4. This system makes checkout very simple and also allows for easy markdowns as the sale progresses. Pink-tagged items might start out at $8 each, be reduced to $5, then $3, and finally to $1.50. Rather than re-mark each item or change the signs at each table, the volunteers need only change the signs on the walls and the lists at the checkout.

One school formerly used a system similar to this one but abandoned the series of markdowns when it instituted the "bag-it sale" (a bag of items for $4 or $5). Revenues didn't fall, and the cashiers' lives became much easier.

STEP-BY-STEP PLANNING AND PREPARATION FOR USED SPORTING GOODS SALE

Stage One (Six Months Before)

Begin planning your sporting goods sale early, as it requires a lot of organization. Once the planning is done, though, you'll find that the sale itself requires very little volunteer time. You'll need to select a date and place for your sale, making sure you're not in competition with any similar sales nearby. The school gym or cafeteria, or any large, secure indoor area, will serve nicely as a location for your sale.

Decide what kind of sporting goods to sell. An elementary school in Schenectady, New York, sells used gear for football, baseball, golf, tennis, swimming, snorkeling, skating, skiing, and bicycling. In addition, it sells baby equipment and large toys such as plastic kitchens and climbing sets. (Other schools that have this type of sale sell children's dress shoes as well.)

You'll also need to decide whether to sell on consignment. The Schenectady school runs its annual sale on consignment, with the PTO keeping 25 percent of the proceeds and the sellers 75 percent. (The total raised each year is about $2,000.)

In addition to an overall chair, you'll need to find people to head the following subcommittees:

publicity
setup and cleanup
volunteers
finance

Stage Two (One to Two Months Before)

PUBLICITY

About a month and a half before the sale, send a flier home to parents letting them know that the sale is coming up. (A sample flier appears at the end of the chapter.) They can then gather the things that they'd like to sell and mark the date on their calendars. Ask for volunteers in the same flier, including a tear-off sheet on which interested parents can choose a time slot for volunteering.

Most schools that have sports sales allow all local residents, not just parents of children attending the school, to sell goods. They put a notice to that effect in the local newspaper about a month before the sale, telling people when and where to drop off their merchandise.

Ads should be submitted for the "garage sale" column of

the classified section of your newspaper and should appear right before the sale. If you have a community newspaper that's distributed free to all households and devoted entirely to advertising, place an ad there as well. This is the time to find out the procedure for placing the ads and write the copy.

VOLUNTEERS

Enlisting volunteers for a sports sale shouldn't be too difficult, because the sale lasts only twenty-four hours from setup to cleanup. At the Schenectady school, which has a student body of about 400, the sale is run with a minimum of volunteers. "We never have trouble finding volunteers, because we let them buy in advance of the sale's official opening," says Marcia Hahnenberger. Two shifts of eight volunteers set up Friday afternoon, and fifteen volunteers man one-and-a-half-hour shifts on Saturday morning.

When you receive the tear-off sheets on the fliers that you've sent home to parents, you'll have a good idea of how many volunteers you have and how many you still need to recruit. If your school has had a similar sale in the past, call people who volunteered then to see if they're willing to come in this time. If you still need more volunteers, call room parents and ask each one to find a few people willing to help out.

FINANCE

Figure out what system you'll use for keeping track of who's owed what at the end of the sale. Here's a simple system that works well:

On Friday as each seller brings in goods he'd like to sell, a volunteer first looks them over to make sure that they're in salable condition.

Then she asks the seller to complete a "code sheet." On it, the seller records his name, address, and phone number and lists and briefly describes each item that he'd like to sell and the price he is charging. At the bottom of the form he signs a statement explaining how the proceeds of the sale will be divided between the school and him and stating that the school is not responsible for lost or damaged items. The volunteer assigns the seller an ID number, which she writes at the top of the form. (A sample code sheet appears at the end of the chapter.)

You might want to add two statements to the code sheet, with a space for the seller to sign his or her name in consent:

1. I give permission for my goods to be sold at half price at 10:30 A.M.
2. I understand that if my merchandise is unsold at the end of the sale, it will be donated to charity.

Sellers then fill out price tags for their items. The price tags are made of heavyweight yellow paper and measure about two and a half inches by three and a half inches. The tags list the seller's name and ID number, the item's size and price, and a brief description of the item (helpful in the event that the tag becomes separated from the item). The tags are attached to the items using duct tape.

A volunteer makes out an envelope for each seller, marking the front with the seller's ID number and name. The envelope will be used to collect the tags of that seller's items that have sold, along with the money he is due.

On the day of the sale, the check-out tables are set up at the doors. When a shopper goes to the cashier with the merchandise that she'd like to buy, a volunteer takes off the price tag(s) and records the seller ID number(s), price(s), and a description of the item(s) on a master code sheet. The price tags are all stored in a shoe box.

In a separate room nearby an accounting crew is at work throughout the sale so that the entire task of figuring out what is owed to whom is not left until the sale is over. Someone from the accounting crew goes to the checkout periodically to collect the price tags from items that have been sold. She takes the tags back to the accounting room, where they're sorted by ID number into the sellers' envelopes.

At the end of the sale, to determine what each seller sold, the accounting crew need only pull the code sheet and envelope for that ID number. It's a simple matter at that point to take the price tags from the envelope, transcribe the sale prices from each price tag onto the code sheet, and add up the column of figures indicating the total owed to the seller. The total is then marked on the envelope, and the envelope is given to a money person, who deposits in it the total sum owed to that seller.

Checklist of items you'll need:

code sheets for each seller

price tags

master code sheets for checkout

printing calculators or adding machines

cashboxes

start-up change

legal-size envelopes

stamp for endorsing checks

slips for making deposits at the bank

sales tax chart if needed

Stage Three (Two Weeks Before)

PUBLICITY

Send a reminder notice home with the students. This is the time to place ads in the newspaper. Pictures are really helpful.

VOLUNTEERS

Remind volunteers by postcard or telephone call of the shifts they've agreed to work.

Stage Four (the Day Before)

SETUP

Setup at the school could be Friday afternoon. As people bring in merchandise, volunteers inspect each item to make sure that it's in salable condition. They do not accept old ski equipment—lace-up boots, for instance, or boots that lack ski brakes. In the flier advertising the sale, parents have been forewarned that ski equipment must be serviceable and have a DIN number (a spring setting based on the skier's height, weight, and ability).

Volunteers have the sellers complete the paperwork described above, pricing each item and affixing the price tags. At the Schenectady school, the sale is held in the cafeteria. As the goods come in, they are grouped by category. Skis are put on tables, and other items are displayed on benches and tables. Two check-out tables are set up near the door.

Once everything has been set up, a presale for the volunteers is held from 8:00 to 9:00 P.M.

Stage Five (the Day of the Sale)

The sale is open for only two hours—9:00 to 11:00 A.M. on Saturday morning. "A few hours is enough," observes Marcia Hahnenberger of Schenectady. "All of the action takes place in the first hour to hour and a half." Some volunteers are stationed at posts, such as at skis; others roam the room, ready to answer questions and making sure that customers don't change price tags; others are cashiers; and still others act as bookkeepers in a separate room.

CHECKOUT

When each item is brought to the cashier, its tag is removed and information about the sale is entered onto a master code sheet.

Sellers may pay by cash or check. As they leave, a volunteer checks to ensure that all tags have been removed.

ACCOUNTING

By the time the sale closes, much of the bookkeeping has already been done, and all that remains is the tallying of totals for each seller. A volunteer adds up the totals on each seller's code sheet, and someone doublechecks the work. A "banker" then puts in each envelope the total amount due to each seller.

PICKUP

At the Schenectady sale, people can pick up their cash and unsold merchandise from 12:00 to 1:00 P.M. When a seller presents himself, a volunteer gives him his cash envelope. Then he claims his unsold merchandise.

CLEANUP

Most people claim unsold merchandise, leaving very little to be disposed of. (At a larger clothesline sale, allowing owners to claim unsold goods would be onerous.) The high school ski team in one community was given unsold merchandise and held its own garage sale.

BANKING

The proceeds of the sale must be deposited in the bank, with statements documented and records maintained. Depending on how much money the school takes in and how many hours the sale is open, several deposits per day might be necessary. At one school orange cones are used to reserve a few parking spaces for people who shuttle back and forth to the bank to make deposits.

Stage Six (a Few Weeks After)

Share the news of the sale's success with parents, faculty, other staff, and the principal. Thank the volunteers in the PTA newsletter, and send notes thanking them personally. Dawn Gehrke, chair of the clothesline sale near Rochester, New York, says, "Personal thank-you notes from the chairman are a social grace but are mandatory to keeping the process in place." She also suggests thanking the physical education teachers and anyone else who's been displaced as a result of the sale.

Finally, make notes concerning what went well and what you'd like to change next time. Convene a final meeting of the committee to discuss how the sale went, and ask each subcommittee chair to submit a report for the school's records.

━━━━✳━━━✳━━━✳━━━

LINCOLN SCHOOL PTO
WINTER SPORTS AND TOY SALE

Dear Parents:

Sell your old skis, ski boots, ice skates, hockey equipment, football and baseball gear, golf and tennis equipment, swimming and snorkeling sets, bicycles, roller skates, skateboards, boogie boards, and other sporting goods. Sell winter outerwear such as boots, snowsuits, jackets, and skiwear. Sell large toys such as strollers, kitchen sets, riding toys, sliding toys, Fisher-Price (and other brand) sets, and children's furniture. Small toys such as puzzles, games, building sets, small dolls and figures, and collections accepted if grouped and sealed in see-through plastic bags.

All ski equipment must be serviceable and have a DIN number.

SELLER GETS 75 PERCENT   PTO GETS 25 PERCENT
DONATIONS WELCOME

Register items: Friday, October 18, 4:00—8:00 P.M.
Sale: Saturday, October 19, 9:00—11:00 A.M.
Pick up cash and unsold items after sale from 12:00—1:00 P.M.

We need volunteers to work at the sports sale. If you're willing, please submit the tear-off form below to school. Volunteers can shop at the sale before it opens to the public.

• •

Yes I'd be happy to volunteer at the sports sale.

☐ Friday, October 18, 3:45 - 5:45 P.M.

☐ Friday, October 18, 5:45 - 8:00 P.M.

☐ Saturday, October 19, 8:45 A.M. - 10:15 A.M.

☐ Saturday, October 19, 10:15 A.M. - 11:45 A.M.

☐ Saturday, October 19, 11:45 A.M. - 1:15 P.M.

Name _____

Phone Number_____

SAMPLE CONSIGNMENT SALE CODE SHEET

Name _____   Seller ID No. _____

Address _____

_____

Phone _____

ITEM DESCRIPTION/SIZE	PRICE	SOLD	25% PTO	75% SELLER
			Total	

The above items have been placed on consignment with the Lincoln PTO. If sold, the PTO will retain 25 percent and I will receive the balance. I understand the PTO is not responsible for loss or damage of the items but will do its best to prevent these. I accept the terms of the sale.

_____
Signature

I have received the TOTAL amount of money for items sold by the Lincoln PTO.

_____
Signature

CHAPTER FIVE

IDEAS FOR MERCHANDISE SALES

WHEN MOST PEOPLE THINK OF PTA FUND-RAISING, THEY THINK of sales of one sort or another—candy, wrapping paper, magazines. Few subjects elicit such strong responses from parents, pro and con.

Brenda Stockton-Hiss of Oklahoma City says: "I, for one, am tired of my kids being asked to sell overpriced wrapping paper, mediocre cheese and sausage products, and candy bars. I'd rather bake cookies, ladle chili, flip pancakes. I'd rather BE there, actively earning the money for the kids' needs, than see them unhappy because everyone's dieting and won't buy candy, hasn't enough money for a $6 roll of wrapping paper, and has already been burned on funny-tasting cheese spread."

"You can never please everyone," comments Kathy Borges of Massachusetts. "One person complained that the gift wrap was overpriced, but another said that she felt better selling something to friends rather than asking for a pure donation for a walkathon, for instance. So we're offering a variety of fund-raisers and emphasizing that we don't want to put any pressure on the kids. People can *choose* which ones they support."

HOW A MERCHANDISE SALE WORKS

You can run a candy, magazine, or wrapping paper sale with a minimum of volunteer effort and often raise large sums of money. A 250-student school in New England sold wrapping paper for the first time—$6,000 of it—for a profit of $3,000.

The company that the school worked with, Genevieve's Gift Wrap, provided the materials for taking orders; each child received an order form along with a brochure containing samples of the wrapping paper. The PTO sent home its own flier explaining the program.

For the most part, the paper cost $6 per roll for fifty square feet. (This is more per roll than you'd pay in a drugstore, but since each roll has much more paper, the price works out to be about the same.) There was a nice selection of recycled paper for Christmas, birthday, and all-occasion use, one Hanukkah paper, as well as ribbon, cards, and recycled stationery.

When the order forms came in, PTO members had to doublecheck the calculations on each form, total the figures, and make sure that each child had collected the correct amount of money. They bundled the orders by classroom and forwarded them to the company. About five weeks later, the wrapping paper was delivered. Each child's order arrived boxed in an individual carry carton. The PTO sent parents a letter saying that the paper would be sent home with the children unless the parents wanted to pick it up themselves or the box was too heavy for the child.

WHAT SHOULD YOU SELL?

It's a good idea to sell something that people would want to buy anyway. Many people buy plants in the spring, for instance, so a Mother's Day plant sale is usually a big hit. In the fall, when people are doing holiday shopping, you can sponsor a craft sale or sell wrapping paper, candy, or other gift items. You can sell school T-shirts any time of year.

Bridget Krowe of New York sums up her philosophy this way: "I think the PTA should either sell something that parents would buy anyway for the same price or less *or* something that promotes the kids' self-esteem or school spirit." She likes sales of magazines, school T-shirts and baseball caps, and calendars featuring artwork done by the students themselves. Magazine sales appeal to her because they have the potential to raise thousands of dollars at a school of a few hundred students, there's no product to deliver, and parents can purchase or renew subscriptions at the same price they would normally pay.

Here are a few ideas for sales. They are described in greater detail later in the chapter (see pp. 81–97). These include:

Mother's Day plants
pies, pizza, or submarine sandwiches
note cards or calendars with children's artwork
videotapes of children's performances
cookbooks
holiday gifts for children to purchase
crafts
family portraits
school T-shirts
school supplies

Some of these sales could become annual events. Others—such as a cookbook sale—could be done only occasionally, during a special anniversary year, for example.

Selling a product such as wrapping paper, magazines, or candy is simple and straightforward, because the company that you deal with supplies just about everything you need, from brochures to letters and forms. (A partial listing of companies and the products they sell appears on pp. 105–8.)

The Step-by-Step Planning and Preparation section (pp. 98–104) gives details about organizing a Mother's Day plant sale.

PRICES

People who buy through a charity are willing to pay a small premium because they know the proceeds go to a good cause. Prices beyond a certain point, however, discourage sales and embarrass the seller. One father brought to work the brochure from the candy sale sponsored by his children's school and took orders totaling $300. When the candy arrived, he was so embarrassed by how meager it looked for the price that he didn't want to deliver it. He claims that he'll never sell that particular line of candy again.

Be very careful in selecting the company that you work with, regardless of what you're selling. Keep in mind that an item that looks wonderful in a slick brochure might turn out to be merely a lot of attractive packaging when you actually see it.

Candy sales need not be disastrous. Sales of inexpensive candy bars can work well for schools regardless of the affluence of the community. Students are given a box of $1 candy bars to sell and asked to bring back the money once they've sold the candy. People who might not have $6 to buy a roll of wrapping paper might have $1 for a candy bar. Bill Russell of Alabama makes this point very well:

> Our school is now trying to sell high-priced ($6–$8) items. The people in this area (including myself) cannot afford these prices. When we sold candy, I could take it to work. I was able to sell to fellow employees. Several times I sold more than one carton! I don't know what profit was made. However, when I take this high-priced stuff out to try to sell it, I get a *lot* of sales resistance. It's too expensive. What I'm trying to say is, don't forget the candy! Unfortunately, my school won't sell it, and unfortunately I won't sell their higher-priced "gifts." So we both lose.

PROFIT MARGIN

Do careful comparison shopping when deciding what to sell. Many companies allow the school to keep 50 percent of sales. You should think long and hard before agreeing to sell something in exchange for only 10 to 20 percent of the proceeds. If the company offers you a sliding scale of profit that increases with your sales volume, be realistic about how much you expect to sell. Always check to see if shipping charges will be billed to the school, or if shipping is free.

Kathy Borges recommends telling parents what the "profit" margin is. "Perhaps they won't mind a $6 roll of wrapping paper, for instance, when they realize $3 is really a donation and the company is getting only $3 for fifty square feet."

SELLING DOOR-TO-DOOR

Most schools discourage children from selling door-to-door. Instead, they recommend selling to family, friends, and neighbors. Some parents don't like their children to be involved in selling, preferring to sell the fund-raising items themselves or not at all.

COLLECTING MONEY

If your school is working with a company selling gift wrap, magazines, food, or anything else through a catalog, the company will either require payment at the time the orders are placed or allow money to be collected when the goods are delivered to customers. Whatever the company's policy, you should require that orders be prepaid: that children turn in money along with their orders. Otherwise, your school runs the risk of having to pick up the tab for potentially large sums of money. (Some schools don't require prepayment on the theory that they sell more and make more money that way, even after deducting amounts that they never collect. Tracking down payments can be a real nuisance, however, and why take such a risk with PTA funds?) The only possible exception to this rule concerns sales of $1 candy bars.

SHOULD YOU OFFER INCENTIVE PRIZES?

Most companies in the business of fund-raising sales push their incentive programs. They claim that sales increase dramatically when children can earn prizes based on the amount they sell. Each child receives a slick brochure picturing the prizes associated with each level of sales, and usually the company offers to launch the sale with a kick-off assembly at which one of its employees promotes the prize program.

Nearly all children wind up earning very inexpensive, carnival-type prizes such as plastic "squeeze-bottles," visors, sunglasses, pens, or the latest inexpensive balls or yo-yos. Selling an extra $50 of goods typically entitles a child to select a gift worth a dollar or two more. For sales of nearly unattainable amounts, children are told they could earn very expensive prizes, such as bicycles.

When schools offer a prize program, the effect of the assembly and the glossy brochures is exactly as intended: Children become intent on selling enough to earn a coveted prize. Often parents react negatively to the incentive prizes and the effects they have on their children. A Florida mother of four puts it this way: "The fund-raisers are driving me crazy. The kids are offered tremendous prizes for the best sales, but they are not to go door-to-door. Pardon my bluntness, but give me a break! Company policy does not allow my husband to sell this stuff at work, and I won't allow my kids to sell door-to-door, so they don't have a chance. To make matters worse, especially in these times, the PTOs are selling items I don't NEED at inflated prices."

Although companies encourage you to offer a prize program, you have the option of not doing so. When a parent group at one school sold wrapping paper, for instance, they could have kept 50 percent of their sales had they chosen to offer prizes. As it was, they didn't offer prizes and were able to keep slightly more—52.5 percent of sales. If you are considering whether to offer a prize program, ask the company for samples of the prizes, just as you would always want to see samples of the product.

If you don't mind the notion of giving prizes but you don't want to give away items that could break easily or otherwise end up in the trash, consider offering your own prizes—school T-shirts or gift certificates for your school's book fair or carnival. You could even offer a limo lunch to a group of top sellers. Rent a limo for an hour, and serve lunch from a fast-food restaurant.

Dawn Heflin of Pennsylvania proposes this fun prize: Allow students to grab a fistful of change from a money jar. She also suggests that everyone who participates be given a pencil and that students who sell to twenty-five customers have their names entered in a raffle for a grand prize, such as a bicycle. If they sell to twenty-five more, their name is entered a second time.

You might decide to reward the *class* rather than the *individual* with the most sales. You can reward the class that sells the most with a popcorn or pizza party.

DELIVERY OF ORDERS

Try to find a company that will deliver each child's order presorted into its own bag or box or shipped directly to the purchaser's home. Otherwise, PTA volunteers will be faced with the mammoth undertaking of sorting the orders. Parents became irate at one school the first year that the PTA sold wrapping paper. The PTA hadn't realized how time-consuming it would be to sort the orders, and volunteers were trying to fill each order as the parents reached the front of what turned out to be a very long line! Presorted orders are definitely worth considering, even if they slightly reduce your school's profit margin.

NOVEL IDEAS FOR THINGS TO SELL

Although most schools sell wrapping paper, magazines, or gift foods—cheeses, nuts, and candy—you don't have to limit your-selves to those items. Descriptions of some less common ideas follow.

Mother's Day Plant Sale

A 250-student public elementary school in St. Louis makes about $4,000 each year selling annuals, potted plants, and hanging baskets at its spring plant sale. About a month and a half before the plant sale, an order form is sent home to parents. Parents place their orders and can then either pick up their plants at school or pay $5 for delivery. (Delivery is free on orders over $75.)

Margot Bean, active with the school's parent association, explains: "Plant orders are all done on computer. The plant sale takes a lot of work, and the chairperson must be very organized and familiar with a computer. Plant pickup is scheduled for one afternoon. The plants are delivered the night before, and the next morning workers split the plants up into orders. This is all done on the playground, which can be locked up at night. The weather usually cooperates but could be a potential problem. We have little plants that the kids can buy. Cactus are big sellers, and so are the little wonder miniature plants."

A school in Poughkeepsie, New York, recently had its first Mother's Day plant sale. It earned $1,200 selling both to parents and the 500 children at the school. Each class visited the sale for twenty minutes, and children were able to buy their mothers plants ranging in price from twenty-five cents for one petunia or marigold to $13 for a big hanging basket.

According to Diane Winkler, who chaired the plant sale, "It was heartwarming to see the children so enthusiastic about the gifts they were buying."

Some children zeroed right in on what they wanted—the small hanging baskets and corsages being the first to go. (Anything with showy pink flowers sold well!) Second-grade Lydia spent $7—$2 that her dad had given her plus $5 of her $7 life's savings—to buy her mom a small hanging basket and corsage. Michael, by nature more deliberative, circled around for the full twenty minutes trying to find the very best plants for his $3. Some children even bought tomato plants for their moms. One kindergartner said, "I hope this tomato plant works. The ones last year did."

After each child paid (some all in pennies and nickels, one with a dollar bill that was bright pink, having been drenched by some Hawaiian Punch in a lunch box), a volunteer put the plants in bags, so the children could carry them home. Some classes made Mother's Day cards, which were stapled to the bags. One teacher had her class use Popsicle sticks to make wishing-well planters that each held a little plant.

Some kids couldn't wait the two days until Mother's Day

and presented their mothers with their plants right away. Others hid their plants—who knows where?—until Mother's Day itself. Odile Matthys's son hid her geranium in his bedroom, watering it profusely every day. She had to sneak in periodically to mop up the puddles. When he asked worriedly, "You haven't seen my surprise, have you, Mom?" naturally she denied everything.

The Poughkeepsie school didn't take preorders. The nursery that supplied the plants had done similar sales before at other schools and so had a rough idea of what to deliver: tomato plants, herbs, and flowers (impatiens, geraniums, pansies, marigolds, and so forth).

The nursery delivered the plants the Wednesday afternoon before Mother's Day. PTA workers set up the plants on tables in the gym and were ready for business on Thursday morning. The sale ran during school hours on Thursday and Friday and for two hours on Thursday evening.

The nursery took back unsold plants at the sale's close.

For detailed information on planning and preparing for a Mother's Day plant sale, refer to pp. 98–104.

Pies, Pizza, and Submarine Sandwiches

How about selling pies for Thanksgiving, pizza on back-to-school night, or submarine sandwiches on Super Bowl Sunday? You can work with a local bakery, placing a large order in exchange for a share of the profit, and then have parents pick up their Thanksgiving pies at school. (Make sure to sell by preorder so that you don't wind up with a lot of pies left over!) On back-to-school or open-house night, when most families are too rushed to sit down to a formal dinner, you can arrange for a pizzeria to deliver pizzas to the homes of school families in exchange for a share of the sale amount.

If you're slightly more ambitious, have volunteers take orders for submarine sandwiches and make them up themselves, in a production line, on Super Bowl Sunday. Or follow the lead of many Midwest schools and sell pizzas that volunteers have assembled. A St. Louis school made over $4,000 from its pizza sale recently.

In St. Louis, several companies supply ingredients for making pizzas. Says Margot Bean, a school mother:

> We pick a date a few months in advance and schedule it with the company. We presell pizzas for about two weeks, turning the order in midweek. On Friday afternoon the supplies arrive, and everything is set up in the cafeteria. Saturday morning the workers arrive at 8:00 A.M. The pizzas are assembled in an assembly line from 8:00 to 12:00 and carried to the gym. People pick up the pizza orders in the early afternoon. The whole affair is lots of fun and a good way for parents to meet one another.

A flier and pizza order form, modeled after this school's forms, appear at the end of the chapter.

Note Cards and Calendars

What parent could refuse to buy note cards or a calendar featuring a picture drawn by his or her own child? When a school in Montclair, New Jersey, sold note cards, about half of the students ordered them, for a total of $5,000 in orders and $3,000 in profit. Linda Lendman, whose son, Zak, is a student, says, "I bought the note cards to give to all of our close relatives for the holidays. I thought it was a great idea."

Lynda Baccoli, vice president in charge of fund-raising for the Montclair school's PTA, notes that "the whole project can be done in about six weeks—start to finish."

During one week, the art teachers had the students each draw a black-and-white picture on an eight-and-a-half-by-eleven-inch sheet of heavy white paper with a black border. Using black fine-point Sharpee markers, the students drew pictures, titled and signed them. The art teachers collected the artwork for each class in a manila folder.

Each child's drawing was assigned a number. For instance, Alice Adams, a student in Mrs. Peter's class, would be P-1, and the next student in that class would be P-2. A volunteer put a sticker with each child's number on the back of his or her drawing.

The PTA reduced the size of the drawings to three and a half inches by five inches and sent each child home with an order form and a copy of his or her picture. Parents could order packs of six note cards of the same design for $5.

The PTA shopped around and contracted with a local printer, who charged $7 per child to make a plate for each drawing and thirty-three cents per card. Once all orders were in, the PTA turned them over to the printer.

The following was "handwritten" on the back of each card:

Artwork by ———

from ——— School

Montclair, New Jersey

It took the printer about a week to print the note cards. The PTA performed the time-consuming task of folding them and putting each set of cards and envelopes in a Ziploc plastic bag that was then sealed with a heart-shaped sticker and tied with a ribbon. Finally, the orders were collated by classroom and delivered to school to be sent home with the children.

Much simpler to organize, but potentially less marketable, are note cards that are not individualized. A Hebrew day school in upstate New York sold packages of Jewish New Year cards bearing unsigned color drawings by students. Each pack contained the same assortment of cards.

An elementary school in Danbury, Connecticut, sold packs of ten assorted color note cards for $5.00. Many parents bought them for their children's thank-you notes. The supplier who prints the school newspaper gave the PTO a discount and ran off about 100 packs of ten. After a few years, the PTO reduced the price to $2.50 per pack to sell the remaining stock. On the back of each note card was printed: "This card was created by the students of ——— Elementary School. All proceeds go toward the support of school activities."

Some schools publish calendars featuring drawings made by students and listing school holidays, concerts, and other special events. A 500-student school in a suburb of New York made a $600 profit one year from a calendar that featured artwork of each child in the school.

In September, the art teacher gave each child a small piece

of paper (one-quarter of a standard sheet of paper measuring eight and a half inches by eleven inches) and a black marker and asked him or her to draw and sign a picture. One class, or sometimes two classes, of children were assigned each month and given a theme: snowmen and winter for January, for instance, and hearts and flowers for February.

PTA volunteers reduced the pictures and made a collage for each month with them, with the overflow on a few extra pages and the covers. They hired a local printer, who charged them about $1.50 per calendar, and they sold 400 at $3 each. The calendars went on sale right after Thanksgiving, making a very nice gift for grandparents for the holidays.

Videotapes of School Productions

The PTA at a school in New Jersey hires a professional to videotape school performances and sells copies of the tape to parents. Over the course of a year, the PTA makes about $900 from the video sales.

Even parents who own their own video cameras like to buy the tapes, because the quality is generally better than what they can produce on their own. The videotaper is a professional who checks the lighting and sound systems. In addition, parents who buy the tapes can sit back and enjoy the show without feeling that they're missing it themselves or blocking the view of parents sitting behind them.

Early in the school year, the PTA contracts with a studio to tape the year's five performances. (Each of the 620 students appears in one performance a year.) The PTA pays the videotaper $125 per show—to watch the dress rehearsal and then to tape the actual performance the next day—and agrees to purchase a minimum of twenty copies of the resulting tape at a cost of $10 per copy.

The PTA sends an order form home to parents a couple of weeks before the performance. Charging parents $16 per tape, the PTA typically sells forty to sixty tapes of a performance featuring 100 children.

The videotaper is paid his $125 on the day of taping. About a week after the performance the PTA places its final order; upon delivery of the tapes (about two weeks later), the PTA pays him for them.

Each videotape comes with a limited warranty from the PTA, stating that parents have seven days in which to preview the tape to ensure that it works well. Over the course of a full year, of the more than 200 tapes sold, only one was returned.

Examples modeled after the PTA's agreement letter, order form, and limited warranty are presented at the end of the chapter.

Cookbook

Although you wouldn't want to publish a cookbook every year, doing so every few years is a great idea. It's much less work than you'd expect, and it's great to have a cookbook with your friends' favorite recipes. Many companies publish cookbooks for church, synagogue, and school groups, and they've made the job easy for you. (For a partial listing of such companies, see p. 106.) Most cookbooks are spiral-bound, with dimensions of five inches by eight and a half inches, and come with standard features, such as dividers, household hints, and indexes.

A 230-student parochial school in New York collected recipes from parents and published a cookbook. The publisher charged $2.50 each for the 400 copies printed, and over the course of a year the PTA sold about 350 books at $6 a copy, for a profit of $1,100.

You need to plan ahead when publishing a cookbook. The interval from the time you first send out letters asking for recipes to the time you receive the finished cookbooks can be three to five months, depending on the season. To sell cookbooks in the most popular months of November and December, then, you probably need to have collected the recipes before school lets out in June.

Mary Ellen Albarino, who was in charge of the cookbook for the New York school, reports that letters were sent home asking for recipes in mid-January; recipes were delivered to the publisher in mid-February; and finished books arrived at the school in mid-April, three weeks before Mother's Day. Parents sold the bulk of the cookbooks. They bought copies for themselves, gave them as gifts to Grandma for Mother's Day, and took them to work to sell to office colleagues. School policy prohibits children from selling door-to-door, so students were not involved in the selling process at all. Mary Ellen took a stack of cookbooks with her everywhere she went for a few months, selling them after church on Sunday, at the school concert, and even at the town's sidewalk sale—wherever the opportunity presented itself.

"It was so easy," says Mary Ellen. "I'm a single mother with three young kids. This [project] appealed to me because it didn't require me to be at school for an extended period of time. I was able to do most of the work at home. I also felt it was a community-building experience. We have a potluck supper every year, and when everyone was commenting about how delicious the food was, I thought of publishing a cookbook. Everybody has a recipe that they're proud of. We collected 246 recipes, and the cookbook is wonderful!"

When you create your cookbook, ask parents, teachers, staff, and even local celebrities and restaurants to submit recipes. If you've had a school event like a potluck supper, suggest that parents submit those recipes. A school with a multiethnic population had sponsored an international dessert buffet, and many of the parents wanted to know how to make the desserts. The cookbook is a perfect opportunity to share those recipes. When a school in Washington, D.C., published its cookbook, recipes included popular foods served at school: a muesli snack and the birthday cake that the cooks make at school.

Although each company that publishes cookbooks works somewhat differently, the basic principle is the same. The company provides forms for parents to use to record their recipes. Each student takes home to his or her parents a few blank recipe forms along with a letter telling about the cookbook. Parents are asked to write neatly or type their recipes on the forms and state the appropriate category for each—appetizers, bread and rolls, desserts, and so forth. (You might even include a special category for recipes easy enough for children to make themselves.)

The recipes must be sorted into categories and sent to the company in the order in which they are to appear in the cookbook. The company types and usually proofreads the recipes and gives the school the option of doing its own proofreading as well. (Some companies charge extra if the school does this supplemental proofreading.) Once you return the proofs to the company, it prints the books and sends them to you.

Kathleen Watt, who oversaw publication of a cookbook for a New York school, says, "I made sure to work with a company that allowed me to proofread the recipes, and I did a very careful job of it. Most people contributed family recipes, and I wanted to make sure we got the recipes and the spelling of people's names correct."

You must pay for all the cookbooks that you order. Some companies require a deposit when orders are placed; others ask for half payment within a month after receipt of the cookbooks and half later on; and still others give customers ninety days in which to send in the full payment.

Depending on the company, your school may have the option of designing its own cover and including in the first few pages of the book a picture of the school and some information about it and the PTA. Most companies also allow customers to design their own dividers. Consider using student artwork for the cover and dividers.

Bear in mind, though, that there's an extra charge for custom-designed dividers and covers, as well as for dividers with protruding tabs, large print, a format larger than regulation size, and pages of advertising at the end of the book.

Shipping is usually not included in the price, so consider shipping costs when making price comparisons. Some companies charge for shipping but send forty or so free cookbooks to cover the cost of shipping.

The school is free to set the price of the cookbook, although the company usually helps out by suggesting a price based on the number of recipes that have been collected. (Everyone who submits a recipe wants a copy of the book!) Printing will cost between $2 and $5 per cookbook, depending on the size of the order, the number of recipes submitted, and the special features selected. With 400 recipes, and an order of 500 cookbooks, most companies would charge about $3 per book.

Don't mark up the price too much. At a higher price you'll get more per book, but you'll sell fewer copies. If you set the price at $5 to $7 per book, you'll probably do well. Selling 500 cookbooks at $6 per book, for instance, would amount to $1,500.

You can sell the cookbooks at every school occasion. A book fair is, of course, a perfect place to sell them. You can also send fliers home and take prepaid orders. If you run out of stock, you can always reorder (the minimum reorder is generally 100 books).

Some schools choose to publish their own cookbooks, working with a local printer. The results can be artistic and individualistic, but it can be something of a financial risk to take this approach. One fall, a school in Maryland produced a beautiful, homey cookbook of its own. According to treasurer Peter Karpoff, "It was a labor of love for the parents." Each page featured one recipe, a few sentences describing it, and a parent-drawn illustration. Five hundred copies of the book were printed at a cost of $3,800, and the selling price was $14.95 per copy. After six months, the school sold 230 copies, but it hoped to sell the lot over three years.

Holiday Shops

A holiday shop is a little store at school where children can make their holiday purchases, selecting from an assortment of inexpensive gift items the PTA sells on consignment. Most holiday shops are not intended to be big money-makers. For instance, an elementary school in Bismarck, North Dakota, has an annual holiday shop that raises a total of $100 to $150. The shop features inexpensive trinkets such as rings, pins, mugs, and pencil sharpeners ranging in price from under a dollar to about $5 for the most expensive item. Goods are marked up 10 percent over their cost. Parents help the children make their selections.

Holiday shops are somewhat controversial. Advocates argue that they provide a wonderful service to both parents and children: Parents are spared the difficult chore of taking their children shopping, and children are taught how to manage their money and provided the opportunity to give as well as to receive at holiday time. Critics point out that it may be difficult to justify forgoing classroom time for shopping, that the shops simply further the commercialization of the holidays, and that they can exclude children who don't celebrate Christmas or don't have the resources to make purchases. Moreover, it's heartbreaking to watch a child's gleeful expression upon presenting a gift turn to sorrow if the gift isn't really appreciated or quickly falls apart. Some parents would rather get a card that their children had made themselves than an inexpensive trinket that they don't really need.

These objections notwithstanding, most of the people who've been involved with holiday shops find the experience rewarding. Dora Rossi of New York City is very enthusiastic about her school's "Christmas boutique," where a variety of items are sold, including Christmas ornaments and dishes.

Although a shop with a Christmas theme may be perfectly appropriate for a private or parochial school, it is not for a public school.

Linda Ritchie, a consultant with Celebrate with Us, a company that supplies the goods for holiday shops, stresses that its shops are always called "holiday" shops (rather than Christmas shops or Santa's workshops) and that many schools try to schedule their sales early enough to precede both Hanukkah and Christmas, even when Hanukkah falls as early as the first week in December. Children who don't celebrate either Christmas or Hanukkah, however, would feel excluded even from such a holiday shop.

Celebrate with Us ships about 100 different items, most of which cost the school between $1 and $2.50. It suggests that schools mark up the prices between 10 and 30 percent. Stock changes every year but usually includes inexpensive boxed jewelry, mugs, scrapers for cars, diaries, sewing kits, key chains, paint or crayon sets, miniature cars, and a number of items labeled "BEST MOM" (or "DAD," "GRANDMA," or "GRANDPA").

Celebrate with Us takes a beginning inventory and delivers everything to the school. The school has to set up the sale. Rather than price items individually, Celebrate with Us recommends grouping items by price and putting price signs on the tables: "MUGS $3" or "ANYTHING ON THIS TABLE $1," for instance. At the end of the sale, the school must take an ending inventory and pack up the unsold goods, which the company will pick up a few days later. Depending on what's left, doing this ending inventory and packing can be quite time-consuming.

An alternative to working with a company that specializes in holiday shops is to take the modest risk of purchasing an assortment of inexpensive gift items outright. What is left over can be saved for next year's shop or given away as prizes at school events.

Volunteers at some schools gift wrap the children's purchases for them. At the Christmas boutique at a school in New York, the PTA sells rolls of wrapping paper, which some teachers buy to help their students wrap their gifts. And at one school in Connecticut, parents prewrap everything that arrives, making sure to keep like items in the same box and to label each box carefully. They keep one of each item out for display. As Sydnye Cohen puts it, "The children then purchase a gift that's already 'hidden' from Mom when they bring it home." The volunteers unwrap all unsold merchandise at the end of the sale before shipping it back to the company.

Crafts

A school facility is large enough to accommodate a craft fair at which individual vendors display their wares on tables. The school can charge a flat rate per table—$25 or so—or a share of the sales—10 or 20 percent. Typically, each vendor collects money individually for what she sells. Even the PTA can set up a table at the fair, selling candy, school supplies, baked goods, or crafts donated by PTA members. Several months before the sale is the time to find vendors. Advertise for them in crafts newsletters and the local paper, and send a note to parents and school employees. Visit craft fairs, asking for business cards of people whose work you like and even asking them if they'd be interested in your school's fair. If more vendors want to come than your school can accommodate, select on the basis of first-come-first-served, or choose school parents and employees first, or simply eliminate duplicates—select just one person to sell dried flower wreaths, for instance.

Once you've selected the vendors, send them each a letter of agreement spelling out financial terms, the day, place, and time of the sale, what the vendor needs to supply (usually his or her own table and chair), how much space he or she will get, and where it will be.

Check with your town or county to determine whether the PTA needs a permit to conduct such a sale and whether it has to hire a police officer to direct traffic. The school might ask the PTA to pay the custodians to clean up after the sale.

Advertise the craft sale to parents by sending home fliers, and invite the public by advertising in the newspaper.

Family Portraits

Some photography studios specialize in taking family portraits as fund-raisers for schools, churches, and synagogues. (See pp. 106–7 for a partial list.) Families typically pay $5 for a family photograph (measuring 10 by 13 inches), and the school gets to keep $4 ($5 if more than a certain number of families participate). In addition, if enough families buy photos, the school gets a cash bonus. At a New York school with 600 students, a photography fund-raiser earned about $1,800 and a VCR for the school. "All in all, it was an excellent fund-raiser," says Ginny Blauvelt, the mother in charge.

The photo session is always scheduled for an evening or weekend. One or two photographers come to the school and set up a studio there. Families are scheduled at ten-minute intervals, and the photographers shoot a series of photographs—a family portrait including at least one adult plus shots of the children together and separately. Some photographers even allow pets to be included, and some have the technology to show the families their pictures right away so there's no need for them to go back to the school another night. In most cases, before the family leaves, they're scheduled for a time two weeks later to come back to pick up their portrait.

When they return for their ten- to fifteen-minute appointment, they're given their family portrait and shown the package including all the other photographs that were taken. The photographs are already developed, so families wanting to purchase them can do so on the spot.

Students at the New York school sold coupons for $5 entitling each family to a group photograph. Most of the people who bought coupons were school families, but some were grandparents, other relatives, and friends of students. The PTA put up some posters around town advertising the event. Children earned incentive prizes such as yo-yos for their sales, which totaled 300 coupons.

The PTA had to schedule times for the 300 families who'd bought coupons to come in and get their pictures taken. The two photographers took pictures at the school all day Saturday, Sunday afternoon, and Monday evening. Three PTA volunteers were on hand at these times, although five would have been better—one to greet people and explain the procedure to them, two to work the check-in table, and two to work the check-out table.

The photographers stuck to their schedule pretty well, and when they got behind the volunteers called people and asked if they could come in a few minutes later. Folding chairs were set up in a hallway as a waiting room, and the photographers worked in the cafeteria.

The photographers were excellent, and they didn't make a hard sell when people came to pick up their portraits. They had a layaway program available for people who couldn't pay immediately. Some people didn't come in for their second appointment, and the photographers simply left the stack of unclaimed family portraits with the PTA. Ginny mailed them to the families.

School Pictures

Some companies that photograph individual children and their classes at school share a part of the proceeds with the PTA. One year an elementary school earned $900 this way—20 percent of all sales.

School T-Shirts

To promote school spirit and maybe make money in the process, many schools sell school T-shirts and sweatshirts, and, less commonly, sweatpants, jackets, caps, visors, banners, and pencils. Friday is sometimes designated as school spirit day, when children are encouraged to wear their school T-shirts. If students (and even teachers) wear their T-shirts when they go on field trips, it's easy to identify them in a crowd.

One school made more than $1,000 selling sweatshirts and T-shirts; another made $200 selling sweatshirts, and later, $200 from T-shirts, shorts, and hats.

T-shirts display the school's name and often a picture as well—of the school, its mascot, or, if you're raising money for a playground, a picture of the playground. Have an adult draw the picture, or sponsor a contest at school and select a child's drawing. Drawings have to be black-on-white (done in black marker or crayon) and close to eight inches by ten inches in size.

Sell by preorder to minimize unsold stock. (Require also that orders be prepaid—you'll have to pay for the T-shirts when you pick them up.) Most companies will make up a sample T-shirt for you to display when taking orders. It's best to get samples in all the different sizes so people know what they're ordering. Be sure to offer both adult and children's sizes; some children wear an adult size, and teachers and parents might want to buy them, too. Display the T-shirt in the school lobby along with the winning picture if your school has had a contest.

Be well organized to keep track of who ordered what. Use order forms on which parents record how many they want of each size and type (T-shirt, sweatshirt, etc.), and total the dollar amount of their orders. Save the order forms so they can be delivered with the T-shirts, and make sure that you've maintained a separate record of your own that you'll be able to refer to in case someone argues that she didn't get what she ordered.

Look in the yellow pages of your phone book under "T-shirts," and phone around to comparison-shop for price and service. The T-shirt business is competitive, so prices ought to be similar and rather inexpensive for bulk orders. Visit the store to see samples of T-shirts prepared for other schools.

Most elementary schools order T-shirts that are 50 percent cotton and 50 percent polyester and done in one color (a light-colored shirt with a darker-colored ink). Companies generally charge a small amount—probably between $15 and $20—to do up a customized design. (This is called a film charge and a screen set-up charge.) Beyond that, they charge for each T-shirt ordered. Note that the larger the order, the lower the price per shirt. For instance, one local store charges a little under $4 per shirt on all orders of more than 150 shirts. On orders of more than 500 shirts, there's no charge for preparation of the design.

Some national companies that sell T-shirts charge more per T-shirt (about $5 per shirt) but provide the customer with order forms and preprinted envelopes to simplify the job of collecting orders and money. They generally don't charge shipping or set-up fees.

Some schools don't expect to make money by selling T-shirts but rather sell them to boost school spirit. They set the price of the shirts just high enough to cover costs. But bear in mind that higher prices do not necessarily lead to higher profits. You might make more profit charging $5 per shirt than charging $10 per shirt. At a higher price, you make more per shirt, but sell fewer shirts!

It's wise to order a few extra shirts in each size, because some people may want to exchange their shirts for a different size, and others will want to buy the shirts once they arrive, even though they didn't preorder them. Reordering shirts is an option, but then you have to pay the set-up charges again. Moreover, on a very small order the per-shirt price is liable to be almost a dollar more than on a large order. If your school runs a store, any leftover T-shirts can be sold there.

Most companies require a 50 percent deposit when orders are placed, with the balance due when customers pick up the T-shirts. It takes most companies about two to five weeks to print the T-shirts.

Ask the company to sort the shirts into boxes by size. It will be much easier to fill each family's order if each size shirt is in its own box. Put each family's order together in its own bag, or tie the shirts with string, and include the order form. One mom reports, "I taped each order form to the appropriate shirt and then put all shirts for one class in a bag, which we delivered to the teacher."

Instead of sending each shirt home with the child who ordered it, send each family's order home with the oldest child in the family. Carol David, who chaired a T-shirt sale, says that this system "reduces your workload substantially."

School Supplies

School stores sell pencils, erasers, rulers, and notebooks to pupils and are usually open for half an hour before school begins in the morning. They afford an opportunity for children to learn about money—as customers spending it wisely, and as store "cashiers" making change.

Although it's possible to make a few hundred dollars a year by operating a school store, this is not a project to be undertaken solely as a fund-raiser. The amount of volunteer time and effort required per dollar of profit is very high. The school store at a Connecticut elementary school raised about $600 over the course of a school year. Ten volunteers took turns staffing the store, which was open for half an hour every morning in October, November, and January through May.

At Halloween, this school store carries masks and creepy rubber toys; before and on Valentine's Day, a variety of valentines; and in the spring, pencils with a bunny theme. All these items sell extremely well. In general, the price of items ranges from ten cents to $1.50. One year, the second-graders who had finished their money unit in math had the privilege of being helpers at the school store. The practice was abandoned because of the logistical problem of getting the children to work before school, but it was a wonderful learning experience for the children involved.

Some schools also sell school folders, featuring the name and mascot of the school on the cover and listing various school and PTA policies and phone numbers on the inside covers. Other schools sell printed "excuse pads" to parents. The school's office staff usually likes them because the forms are all the same size (four inches by five inches) and easy to read and file. Parents simply fill in the line on the pad that fits their particular circumstances: "Johnny was not in school due to _____ ," "will be picked up by _____ ," "will go home with _____ ," "has a doctor's appointment at _____ ," and so forth. Each pad of fifty sheets sells for $1 to $1.25 and costs thirty or forty cents to print.

STEP-BY-STEP PLANNING AND PREPARATION FOR A MOTHER'S DAY PLANT SALE

Stage One (Six Months Before)

Start thinking about a Mother's Day plant sale early enough to give the nursery adequate time to plan how to plant its greenhouse and also, as with any fund-raiser, to clear the project with the principal.

THE COMMITTEE

The person appointed to chair the plant sale should recruit a small group of people to head the following subcommittees:

publicity

liaison with the nursery

liaison with school personnel

finance

volunteers

At the first meeting of the committee, choose a date, aiming for one right before Mother's Day, but checking for conflicts at school. Never schedule a plant sale for a Monday. Teachers should be able to make reminder announcements in class the day before the sale. Decide:

whether to sell to children or only to adults

whether to sell by preorder

where to set up the sale—outdoors or indoors

Should you sell to children? When you consider this question, keep in mind that children absolutely love being able to buy plants for their moms for Mother's Day and continue to be delighted as they watch the plants grow. They love being able to buy something beautiful for a nominal sum, and they love the suspense of hiding their purchases until Mother's Day.

In addition, most mothers are pleased to get a plant as a gift. On the other hand, even if each class visits the plant sale for only twenty minutes, that is twenty minutes of lost classroom time. Moreover, you might be concerned about the children's being able to transport their plants home safely.

Should you take preorders? Selling primarily through preorder has worked extremely well for an elementary school in St. Louis. The school even arranges for orders to be delivered to customers. Some nurseries recommend against taking preorders, however, since one person's notion of a flower of a certain color or species might differ from another's. For instance, someone might order light pink impatiens and complain that what she got was dark pink or coral.

Should you set up the sale outdoors? Setting up a plant sale outdoors keeps the dirt outdoors, but to do so you must be certain that the temperature won't drop below freezing and that you'll be able to secure the plants after hours.

LIAISON WITH NURSERY

At this stage, you need to choose a nursery. Find one that's willing to:

provide healthy plants at a good price

deliver plants to the school and restock if necessary

take back unsold plants at the end of the sale

guarantee adequate stock

Sit down with a representative of each nursery to discuss the type of plant sale that you envision. If children will be included as customers, ask if the nursery could supply you with little plants that would cost under $5—small potted geraniums and begonias, four-inch hanging baskets, and maybe even some inexpensive corsages. For adults, request flats of bedding plants and vegetables and larger, more expensive hanging baskets.

Once you've selected a nursery, work out a written agreement, and sit back and relax for a few months.

Stage Two (One Month Before)

If each class is to visit the plant sale, find a safe way for children to carry home their purchases. Putting each child's plants in a grocery bag ought to guarantee safe transport. Ask each committee member to start saving bags.

To ensure that no child feels bad about not being able to buy his or her mom a plant, be willing to break up six-packs and sell the plants individually to children who have only twenty-five cents to spend. There'll always be some children, though, who will bring in three dollars and want to purchase twelve different plants! Decide what the rules will be.

PUBLICITY

Let parents know about the upcoming plant sale early enough so that they don't buy their plants elsewhere. A few lines in a PTA newsletter or a flier would serve the purpose. (A sample flier appears at the end of the chapter.)

If the sale will be open to the public, write a press release for the local and community newspapers to advertise it.

LIAISON WITH NURSERY

Touch base with the nursery to make sure that you're still on and that everything's growing well.

LIAISON WITH SCHOOL PERSONNEL

Firm up plans for where the sale will take place, what time it will be set up, and how many tables will be needed. Begin thinking about how to minimize the mess if the sale will take place indoors. Laying sheets on the floor underneath each table works well to keep the floor clean.

Even if children will be visiting the sale, holding it over one or two days with a few evening hours ought to suffice. The plants shouldn't sit so long that they need watering.

Let the teachers know about the sale so they can incorporate it into their lesson plans and schedules. Some teachers might have their students make cards or Popsicle-stick planters to go along with the plants. Make sign-up sheets for the teachers to schedule class visits. That way, when you're enlisting volunteer help, you can assign volunteers to be at the sale when their children visit.

Stage Three (One to Two Weeks Before)

Publicity

Send a flier home about two weeks before the plant sale telling parents what will happen at the sale: how children and adults can make purchases, when and where the sale will be held, and what prices will be charged. With this information, parents can be sure that their children go to school with a small amount of money the day of the sale, and they'll know when they can do their own shopping. (A sample flier appears at the end of the chapter.)

Put up some posters or signs around school to advertise the sale. Make whatever signs you'll need at the sale itself.

Volunteers

You won't need many volunteers for a plant sale: Five per shift ought to suffice (two to be cashiers and three to help children make their selections). Gather names, coordinating with the person in charge of publicity. The sample flier just referred to contains a tear-off sheet for volunteers.

Stage Four (One or Two Days Before)

Publicity

Send home a half-page reminder notice so that parents remember to send money in with their children. (A sample flier appears at the end of the chapter.)

Liaison with Nursery

Reconfirm the exact delivery time. Ask the nursery to deliver some wagons that parents and teachers can use to wheel their purchases out to their cars. Arrange to buy enough long-stemmed carnations to give one to each volunteer at the sale.

LIAISON WITH SCHOOL PERSONNEL

Send teachers reminder notices about the times their classes are scheduled to visit the plant sale. Explain overall procedures to them.

Touch base with the custodians to restate the number of tables you'll need and when and where you'll be setting up and cleaning up.

FINANCE

Prepare to bring the following to the plant sale:

two calculators

a cashbox with $30 start-up change

bank deposit slips

scrap paper

scissors

VOLUNTEERS

Call each volunteer to remind her of her time slot, or send each a short note. If you haven't collected enough bags, ask each volunteer to bring some along, or go to a local store to ask for a donation. Make sure to have name tags and a schedule of volunteers on hand at the sale.

Stage Five (the Sale)

SETUP

In setting up the sale, arrange the tables in a horseshoe or donut shape. Lay sheets underneath before you bring in any plants. Display the plants so that vegetables and herbs are together, and flowers are grouped by price: all six-packs together, all four-inch pots together, and so forth. Don't put price tags on every plant; just put signs indicating prices on each table. With plants grouped that way, when a child comes in with a certain amount of money to spend, you can direct him or her to the

right section. It's difficult to display hanging plants; if a porta-
ble coatrack is available, wheel it in and hang plants from it.

Put extra flats and plants underneath the tables so you can
restock quickly.

Set up a cashier table near the door, with a few chairs and
a wastepaper basket.

THE DAY OF THE SALE

As each child makes a purchase, put the plant in a grocery bag
and fold it over or staple it to make it easy to carry home.

Midway through the day, call the nursery to restock if
you're running low on any particular item.

At the end of the day, have the treasurer make a deposit at
the bank, and be sure to lock up.

At the end of the sale, if only a few plants are left, sell
them to the volunteers at your cost. Give each volunteer a long-
stemmed carnation as a thank-you. Clean up as well as you
can, and make sure to thank the custodians. Pay the nursery
bill.

Stage Six (a Week or Two After)

PUBLICITY

In the PTA newsletter, let everyone know how well the plant
sale did.

LIAISON WITH SCHOOL PERSONNEL

Report to the principal about the sale's success.

LIAISON WITH THE NURSERY

Talk to the nursery's representative to discuss how the sale went
and how it could run more smoothly next year.

VOLUNTEERS

Send notes to thank each volunteer.

THE COMMITTEE

Convene a meeting of the entire committee to discuss what worked well and what could be improved next time the school has a plant sale.

———✳———✳———✳———

FUND-RAISING COMPANIES

Here is a partial listing of fund-raising companies. Consult your local yellow pages for names of additional companies.

Candy

Elite Fund Raising, Ltd.
1461-18 Lakeland Avenue
Bohemia, New York 11716
1-800-688-6664
(New York: 1-516-244-7770)

M&M Mars
Fundraising Department
High Street
Hackettstown, New Jersey 07840
1-800-631-7630

Nestle-Beich
P.O. Box 2914
Bloomington, Illinois 61702-2914
1-800-431-1248

Oriental Trading
4206 S. 108th Street
Omaha, Nebraska 68137
1-800-228-2269

World's Finest Chocolate
4801 South Lawndale
Chicago, Illinois 60632
1-800-932-3863

Citrus Fruit

Indian River Citrus Specialties
1155 Louisiana Avenue, Suite 205
Winter Park, Florida 32789
1-800-223-7740

River Star Farms
P.O. Box 846
Weslaco, Texas 78599
1-800-662-8808

Cookbooks

Circulation Service, Inc.
P.O. Box 7306
Leawood, Kansas 66207
1-913-491-6300

Cookbooks by Morris Press
3212 E. Highway 30
P.O. Box 1681
Kearney, Nebraska 68848
1-800-445-6621

Cookbook Publishers, Inc.
2101 Kansas City Road
P.O. Box 1260
Olathe, Kansas 66061
1-800-227-7282

Fundcraft Publishing
P.O. Box 340
Collierville, Tennessee 38027
1-800-351-7822

General Publishing & Binding, Inc.
R.R. 3, Box 163
Iowa Falls, Iowa 50126
1-800-397-8572

Walter's Cookbooks
215 5th Avenue, S.E.
Waseca, Minnesota 56093
1-800-447-3274

Family Portraits

Continental Family Portraits
164½ First Street
Cleveland, Tennessee 37311
1-800-251-6408

Crown Studios
1503 South 169 Highway
Smithville, Missouri 64089
1-800-228-3608
1-816-873-2121

Photo One
9191 E. U.S. 40
Greenfield, Indiana 46140
1-800-233-2494

Holiday Shop and Student Store Items

Celebrate with Us! Inc.
2111 Edgar Road
Point Pleasant, New Jersey 08742
1-908-295-3453

Magazines

QSP (a division of Reader's Digest)
P.O. Box 10203
Des Moines, Iowa 50336
1-800-678-2673

Wrapping Paper

Cherrydale Farms
Rte. 663 and Quakertown Rd.
Pennsburg, Pennsylvania 18073
1-800-333-4525

Genevieve's Gift Wrap Sales
P.O. Box 147
West Springfield, Massachusetts 01090
1-800-842-6656

Great Western Reserve
1310 Starlight Drive
P.O. Box 7653
Akron, Ohio 44306
1-800-666-4136

Innisbrook Wraps
P.O. Box 16046
Greensboro, North Carolina 27416
1-800-334-8461

Sally Foster Giftwrap
P.O. Box 1868
Spartanburg, South Carolina 29304
1-800-237-9727

You are invited to participate in the

FOURTH ANNUAL
LINCOLN SCHOOL

PIZZA SALE

COMING NOVEMBER 1

14" PIZZAS: $5.00-5.50-6.50

PRESALE: OCTOBER 18 - OCTOBER 31

We hope you'll support this fund-raising effort for Lincoln School by planning to order pizzas and by volunteering to help assemble and distribute pizzas. Class prizes will reward the best sales efforts. Look for the preorder forms that will be coming home with your children.

For more information or to volunteer, contact: _____ .

Dinner is served!

Lincoln School Association

FRESH PIZZA

Fourth Annual Pizza Sale

Buyer_____

Address_____

Phone_____

For Office Use Only—Picked up by:

Pizza size—14"

_____Supreme* $6.00   _____Pepperoni $5.50

_____Hamburger $5.50   _____Cheese $5.00

Buy three pizzas, get $1.00 off

Total number pizzas _____

Total amount paid _____

Seller_____Teacher_____Grade_____

Cash or check payable to Lincoln School Association must accompany each order. All orders to be returned by_____.

*INGREDIENTS IN SUPREME: PEPPERONI, HAMBURGER, CHEESE, AND MUSHROOMS

- -

Receipt

Buyer_____ Amount Paid_____

for

_____Supreme _____Hamburger _____Pepperoni _____Cheese

Pickup: School Gymnasium, November 1, Between 1:30 and 4:00 P.M.

PIZZAS NOT PICKED UP ARE CONSIDERED A DONATION.

PTA VIDEO—HOUSE D PERFORMANCE

Dear Parents and Guardians:

Stay tuned for House D's performance of "The Gift from the Sea and the Stars," coming to a theater near you on December 1!

Want to preserve the memories? This one-time-only event will be captured on videotape and yours to enjoy on VHS format for $16! Preorder your tape now and be guaranteed a souvenir of this unforgettable, star-studded show.

Run, don't walk, to fill out the form below and return it with a check or money order to your child's teacher.

Chairperson, Video Project

PTA VIDEOTAPE ORDER FORM: HOUSE D

Parent's name _____ Child _____

Phone _____ Child's teacher _____ Room number _____

Number of tapes _____ × $16 = Amount enclosed _____

Please make your check or money order payable to _____ PTA. Do not send cash. Please put your phone number on the check. Return this order form and your payment to your child's teacher in an envelope marked PTA VIDEO.

Deadline for early orders _____ .

Tapes can also be ordered the day of the performance. Don't forget your checkbooks! Tapes will be distributed on _____ .

LIMITED WARRANTY

NOTE: YOU HAVE 7 DAYS IN WHICH TO PREVIEW THIS TAPE TO ASSURE YOURSELF OF ITS WORKING ORDER. IF YOU HAVE A PROBLEM, CONTACT ME DIRECTLY. <u>DO NOT RETURN THE TAPE TO SCHOOL.</u> AFTER THE DATE BELOW, NO ADJUSTMENT WILL BE MADE.

DATE: _____

CHAIRPERSON, VIDEO PROJECT

SAMPLE AGREEMENT LETTER

Dear _____ :

I'm glad you'll be taping our children's performances at Lincoln School.

As we discussed, we'll pay you $125 for coming to see a dress rehearsal and taping the hour show on the performance day. The performances will be shot on S-VHS. The VHS dubs will cost $10 per copy (that price is for a minimum order of twenty dubs).

Please see the dates of the performances below and reserve them for us. I will call you with the date and time of the dress rehearsal for the October 1 performance.

We look forward to working with you on this project.

Yours truly,

_____

School Peformances

October 1	10:00 A.M.
December 1	10:00 A.M. or 7:00 P.M.
February 1	10:00 A.M.
April 1	10:00 A.M. (please note this date may change)
June 1	10:00 A.M.

Come One and All
PTA Plant Sale
at
Lincoln School

Thursday, May 1, 9:00 A.M.–2:30 P.M. *and* 6:00 P.M–8:00 P.M.
Friday, May 2, 9:00 A.M.–2:30 P.M.

Don't Forget Mom on Mother's Day

Annuals
Perennials
Vegetable Plants
Hanging Baskets
and Much More

WATCH FOR MORE INFORMATION IN THE APRIL

NEWSLETTER

PTA PLANT SALE

WHEN: Thursday, May 1:   9:00 A.M. to 2:30 P.M. and 6:00 P.M. to
                                 8:00 P.M.
           Friday, May 2:   9:00 A.M. to 2:30 P.M.

WHERE: gym

KIDS: Each class will visit the plant sale on Thursday or
Friday (May 1 or 2) so that children can purchase plants for
their mothers for Mother's Day. On Thursday, please send your
child to school with a small amount of money—cash or check made
payable to the Lincoln PTA. Even if children have only fifty
cents, they can buy a very small plant. The plants will be put
in bags so that the children can carry them home.

PARENTS: The PTA is counting on you to come to school to buy
plants for your spring planting needs. We will have a nice
assortment of annuals, hanging baskets, and even some herbs and
vegetables. You may come any time that the sale is open. Note
that we will be open Thursday evening.

VOLUNTEERS: We still need lots of volunteers. If you can help
out, please complete the form below and return it to the PTA box
in the school office or call ————————.

PRICES:

```
Annual Packs (6 plants) . . . . . . . . . . . . $1.50
            include: petunias, impatiens, begonias,
                 marigolds, snapdragons, dusty miller, vegetables
      Herb Plants  (4" pots) . . . . . . . . . . $2.50
      Geraniums  (4" pots) . . . . . . . . . . . $2.50
      Hanging Baskets  (6" kid's special). . . . $4.00
      Hanging Baskets  (8"). . . . . . . . . . . $9.00
            include: ivy, geraniums, fuchsia, petunias,
                 impatiens
```

- -

I'D LIKE TO VOLUNTEER AT THE PLANT SALE.

Name _____

Child's name _____

Child's teacher _____

Phone _____

When I can work _____

PTA PLANT SALE REMINDER!

When: Thursday, May 1   9:00 A.M. TO 2:30 P.M. *and*
                                   6:00 P.M. TO 8:00 P.M.
         Friday, May 2   9:00 A.M. TO 2:30 P.M.

Where: Gym

Kids: Don't forget Mom on Mother's Day!

Parents: Remember to give your kids a small amount of money—cash or a check made payable to the Lincoln PTA—and don't forget to visit the plant sale *any time* the sale is open.

PRICES:

      Annual packs (6 plants) $1.50
      Herb plants (4″ pots) $2.50
      Geraniums (4″ pots) $2.50
      Hanging baskets (6″) $4.00
      Hanging baskets (8″) $9.00

Thanks for supporting your PTA.

CHAPTER SIX

AUCTIONS

A SCHOOL IN SOUTH BEND, INDIANA, MADE $170,000 AT ITS annual auction. Private schools have long relied on auctions, but public schools are increasingly turning to them because of their money-making potential. An elementary school in New-town, Connecticut, for instance, netted $9,000 from a recent auction. Auctioneer Kip Toner claims that a public elementary school organizing an auction for the first time can expect to make at least $10,000, assuming about 200 parents attend and 400–500 items are auctioned. He says that private elementary schools that hold annual auctions typically make between $50,000 and $80,000 from them.

Auctions have the potential to be so profitable because the auction merchandise is donated by local stores, friends of the school, and parents. To be successful, parents have to canvass the community to solicit donations and collect and keep track of hundreds of donated items, while planning the evening of the auction. Organizing a full-fledged auction is an enormous undertaking which you should not attempt without a commit-ted and capable committee of at least fifty volunteers.

Those who have chaired auctions maintain that their work begins six months to a year in advance and occupies them nearly full-time for several months. At one school, work on the auction begins about a year and a half before and is so demand-ing that an auction is held only every seven years. When the chairwoman of a November auction was being interviewed for this book in January, her son overheard her say the word "auction" and started screaming, "Are you working on the auction again already?"

WHAT MOST AUCTIONS ARE LIKE

Most auctions are all-adult, dressy social affairs that mix business with pleasure over dinner or cocktails.★ Some schools rent hotel ballrooms for this purpose, but most simply transform their gyms, promlike, into festive, faraway places decorated in keeping with the evening's theme. Guests pay a cover charge, which, at a minimum, defrays the cost of the meal or party. The auction itself is usually divided into two parts—a silent auction followed by a live auction.

The Silent Auction

The silent auction takes place during the cocktail hour. At their leisure, guests view the merchandise—ideally hundreds of items such as gift certificates, small appliances, crafts, artwork, food, and clothing—displayed colorfully around the room. They record their bids on bid sheets, which are laid out next to each item, and they return periodically to check the sheets and increase their bids when necessary. At the end of the silent auction, the highest bidder on each sheet has bought the corresponding item.

The Live Auction

The most costly and desirable items—airplane tickets, weekend getaways, celebrity donations—are reserved for the live auction. This part of the evening begins after the cocktail hour and typically lasts about two hours. An auctioneer, professional or volunteer, auctions off each of seventy-five to 100 items. While attending to the business of getting the guests involved in the bidding, the auctioneer also entertains. One auctioneer says that he asks parent or teacher volunteers to put on skits for

★An excellent and complete guide to hosting a charity auction is *The Auction Book*, by Betsy Beatty and Libby Kirkpatrick (available from Auction Press, 412 Milwaukee Street, Denver, Colorado 80206).

each item auctioned. "At one school, when I auctioned a week in a condo in Hawaii, two teachers came on stage wearing grass skirts and dancing to Hawaiian music," he reports.

WHERE TO HAVE YOUR AUCTION

The number one consideration in choosing a location for an auction is finding someplace large enough; naturally, as many people as possible should be able to attend. You'll need one room—such as a gym—spacious enough to hold many tables of merchandise for the silent auction and places for people to sit during the live auction. Less desirably, instead of having both the silent and live auctions in the same room, you could have one in the cafeteria and one in the gym. During the live auction, the auctioneer and several other people need to be on a stage or dais so that everyone can readily see them. "We had a hard time finding a location for our auction," says Alana Long. "We couldn't have it at school and serve wine. We wanted it local for fear people wouldn't come otherwise. We found a community center which was rather small, so we had to be very clever when we arranged [the] setup." At Long's school, as each section of the silent auction closed, those tables were cleared of merchandise and converted to another use: first to create tables for checkout and then for guests to sit around during the live auction.

It is possible to rent a ballroom in a hotel or country club, but this alternative could be expensive. Be creative and look for other places that could be used at no cost. One school held its auction in the town hall, and another used the penthouse boardroom of a corporation's headquarters.

WHEN TO HAVE YOUR AUCTION

Weekend evenings in late fall and spring are the most popular times for auctions. Since preparations for an auction begin months in advance, a spring auction allows preparations to begin in earnest in September, whereas much of the work must be done over the summer for a November auction. People are in the gift-buying mood in November, however, so you might raise more money then than in the spring.

WHAT SORT OF EVENING SHOULD IT BE?

Remember that you want to raise money at your auction, but you also want guests to enjoy themselves while getting to know one another better. To make it fun, choose a theme. This lends an air of festivity to the evening and makes it easy to come up with novel decorations, invitations, and programs. If you decide to make an auction an annual event, changing the theme from year to year maintains interest and enthusiasm.

When one school used a safari theme, it adorned its invitations and catalog with drawings of wild animals and even decorated the bidding paddles to look like animal heads. A private school in Massachusetts chose the Grand Prix as a theme. "Anytime I saw something come home from school with a drawing of a race car, I knew it had something to do with the auction," says one of the parents, with a rueful smile.

Themes that school have chosen for auctions include:

African Safari	Fifties or Sixties
Celebration of Spring	Monte Carlo Night
Country Circus	Trip to the Orient
Masquerade	Carnival
"As You Like It"	Mardi Gras
Grand Prix	Winter Festival
Valentine's Day	St. Patrick's Day "Luck of the Bid"

It's a good idea to serve food at your auction, including cocktails if state law permits. In *The Auction Book*, Betsy Beatty and Libby Kirkpatrick recommend having a sit-down dinner as an inducement for people to stay for the entire live auction. If this is your school's first auction, though, simply have a wine and cheese party during the silent auction and coffee and dessert during the live auction. Ask parents to bake desserts, caterers to donate finger food, grocery stores to donate soda, cheese, and crackers, and liquor stores to donate liquor and wine. (Remind vendors that these donations are tax-deductible.)

SHOULD YOU USE A PROFESSIONAL AUCTIONEER?

Most schools tend not to use professional auctioneers, preferring instead to appoint the principal or a gregarious parent or teacher to the job. (In most states, auctioneers who donate their time do not have to be licensed, but you should check the rules in your state.) The volunteer with the right personality can play on his or her friendships with parents to lend an air of jocularity to the evening, as well as to solicit higher bids from certain people: "Come on, Bill, you're not going to let Carol get that lasagna dinner for only $100, are you?"

On the other hand, auctioneers are professionals, and they know how to keep up a steady pace and elicit the highest bids. Sue Hornbeck of Indiana says that proceeds from her school's auction increased tenfold after a proven professional auctioneer was hired both to train the volunteers and to act as the evening's auctioneer.

A professional can auction about seventy-five items over the course of two and a half hours, as compared with the thirty-five or forty items a typical volunteer can do in the same time, according to auctioneer Kip Toner. He claims that items sell for about 20 percent more at a live auction than at a silent one, so those extra items that an auctioneer can move from the silent to the live auction earn that much of a premium.

Auctioneers who specialize in charity auctions tend to be entertainers skilled in making the evening enjoyable and profitable. In addition, they usually sell extremely helpful extras— training sessions for volunteers, paddles, and computer programs and specialized forms—for a fee on top of their standard fee of about $1,500 to $2,500 for an evening. Some auctioneers who don't specialize in charity auctions are willing to donate their time when doing a charity auction, whereas others are willing to do charity auctions for a fee of a few hundred dollars or in exchange for being able to bring a few items of their own to auction. If your school's auction is an annual event, try to use the same auctioneer, for he or she will learn how to "work" your crowd.

STEP-BY-STEP PLANNING AND PREPARATION

Full-fledged auctions that raise tens of thousands of dollars are extremely complicated in conception and execution. Just keeping track of the merchandise is an enormous undertaking. You must solicit, store, and catalog it, transport it to the auction, display it, and ultimately hand it over to the purchaser—all the time keeping meticulous records. In addition, you must plan the evening's festivities—arrange for space, food, decorations, lighting and sound systems, an auctioneer, and check-in and checkout procedures. You must issue invitations and print an auction catalog. In short, planning an auction is more time-consuming than planning a wedding.

Detailing the process of planning and executing an auction can't be done in just one chapter. The remainder of this chapter, therefore, deviates from most other chapters in the book. Instead of a complete step-by-step guide, it presents a logistical overview of the evening of the auction itself and then highlights some of the work leading up to the auction.

Invitations and Catalog

Send invitations, possibly with a list or catalog of what will be auctioned, to entice people to attend to parents, faculty, and business donors. To keep costs down, you can send invitations home with the children, with a tear-off reservation form at the bottom. Encourage people to bring friends along, and ask businesses to purchase tickets for a complete table of guests.

About two weeks before the auction, send catalogs listing all items to be auctioned to everyone who has responded that they'll be attending. Kip Toner suggests enclosing highlighter pens and sticking a Post-it note to each catalog with the following handwritten message: "Don't forget to go through this catalog to mark things that you'd like. Bring it with you to the auction!"

Night of the Auction

CHECK-IN

When they walk into the school gym, guests find themselves in a fantasy world—an African jungle, a winter wonderland, or a tropical paradise, for instance. Soft background music might be playing, and someone is making announcements from time to time. Long tables full of merchandise for the silent auction line the outside of the room, and circular tables are set up in the center of the room where parents will sit during the live auction. A bar is set up near the silent auction (so the merchandise gets good exposure), and waiters circulate with hors d'oeuvres.

A typical timetable for the evening might be:

7:00 P.M.–8:30 P.M.	check-in, silent auction, and cocktails
8:30 P.M.–10:30 P.M.	live auction and dessert
10:30 P.M.–11:30 P.M.	checkout and merchandise claim

Upon checking in at the door, guests are given packets including catalogs, name tags, seat assignments, bid numbers, and paddles. The paddles display each guest's bid number. (A couple gets two paddles, each with the same number.) If you're working on a low budget, forgo the paddles and simply write bid numbers on the back of each catalog. Guests also use their bid numbers when recording bids in the silent auction.

THE SILENT AUCTION

During the cocktail hour, guests circulate through the table area and bid on the silent auction merchandise by recording their bids on "bid sheets" taped next to each item.

What is the best way to display the merchandise? Arrange it on long tables around the perimeter of the room, with a volunteer stationed at each table or each couple of tables. Group everything by type, and display it in numerical order, so that, for instance, all children's items are on one table, numbered C01–C36, and all house and garden items, numbered H01–

H25, on another. With this system, guests can easily find things they've circled in their catalogs at home and relocate items they've bid on to see whether they need to bid more.

Sue Hornbeck gives this advice: "Make the merchandise look great. Add color and dimension with fabric, glistening paper, and old crates and streamers. The more dramatic and vibrant it looks to the bidder, the higher the bid for your school."

Some items can be displayed right on the tables, whereas others are so large that they need to be displayed behind the tables, or so valuable that they should be locked in display cases. Never display an actual gift certificate. Rather, describe the item on posterboard, and illustrate it with photographs to show it to its best advantage. For a gift certificate for use of a vacation house, for instance, post photographs of the house or the view from the front window or, if those aren't available, magazine clippings evoking the atmosphere of the spot.

Next to each item in the silent auction should be taped a bid sheet, attached to which is a pen on a colorful ribbon. The bid sheet provides the catalog number and description of the item and has lines to be filled in with bids. The first line, which states the minimum bid that you'll accept for that item, gets filled in before the night of the auction. An entire subcommittee is usually responsible for pricing—that is, setting the minimum bids and minimum allowable raises for the silent auction. Minimum bids are usually set at one-third to one-half of the item's retail value. A raise is the amount by which one bid exceeds the previous one. For instance, for a toaster-oven, the minimum bid might be $10, and the minimum raise $5. If someone sees that someone else has bid $15 for the toaster oven, she cannot bid less than $20 for it. One school found that it made the most money by setting low minimum bids and large raise amounts. (The school also color coded its bid sheets, so that all items in the same category had the same color bid sheet.)

During the silent auction, as volunteers circulate to bid for themselves, they should check the bid sheets to ensure that proper bid increments have been followed.

Some schools list the retail value of an item on the bid sheet, but others don't, on the theory that people often bid above the value of an item. Some schools have bidders list both their names and paddle numbers on the sheet, whereas others have bidders list only their numbers, because sometimes people don't want to offend friends by bidding against them. (A sample bid sheet appears at the end of the chapter.)

At many schools, the various sections of the silent auction are closed at different times. Announcements are made fifteen minutes before each section closes: "Hurry over to the children's table—Table 2. It's closing in fifteen minutes, and we've just marked down the minimum bid on the scooter to only $15!" It's imperative to announce the closing of each section so there can be no argument about who was the highest bidder at that time.

At the end of the silent auction, the volunteer at each table collects all the bid sheets from her section and delivers them to the cashiers, who are stationed by the exit. They take the bid sheets, fill out individual invoices, and file the invoices by each participant's bid number, so that at the end of the auction, all invoices with the same bid number have already been collated. The bid sheet is returned to its original table area so participants may check to see if they were the highest bidder.

THE LIVE AUCTION

The live auction features the most sought-after goods and is the highlight of the evening. Make it fast-paced, and don't waste time with long speeches, thank-yous, or introductions, or by announcing the winners of the items in the silent auction.

It's imperative that the audience be able to see and hear the auctioneer, so a crew needs to arrange lighting and sound systems in consultation with the auctioneer.

Try to line up volunteers to put on skits for each item being auctioned, as Kip Toner recommends. When auctioning off a day's use of a limo, for instance, he suggests having someone parade around on stage wearing a chauffeur's hat and carrying a steering wheel. If that sort of showmanship sounds too corny or too difficult to stage, put on a slide show instead, or try a combination of the two approaches. At the least, have volunteers walk around displaying the items being auctioned.

You obviously want guests to stay until the end of the

auction, so make sure that they have a good time and that they're alert enough to participate in the bidding. Serving them coffee and dessert helps. Perhaps most important, don't break in the middle. Breaks provide an opportunity for people to leave, and make it difficult to regain momentum. Professional auctioneers recommend having guests sit at tables during the live auction instead of having them sit auditorium-style facing front. At tables people can visit with their friends and eat and drink. Auctioneer Lance Walker says that it's unreasonable to expect guests to sit in silence for two hours or longer.

People are more likely to stay until the end of the auction if you have carefully planned the order in which you present the goods. Beatty and Kirkpatrick suggest beginning with a few items of lesser value, since it takes people a little while to settle down and get into the swing of things. Then stagger the most attractive items throughout the evening, making sure to separate similar items, so that, for instance, season hockey tickets are not presented immediately after season football tickets. (Items from the live auction should be listed in the catalog in the order in which they'll be auctioned.) As an additional means of keeping people until the end, you can announce door prize winners throughout the live auction and wait until the end of the evening to announce raffle winners. If you're raffling a big-ticket item, periodically pull ten names and then, at the end, pull the winner from these forty or fifty.

The bidding process works as follows: People bid during the live auction by raising their paddles. Volunteer "spotters" are stationed around the room to assist the auctioneer in finding bidders. Often the spotters have flashlights to highlight bidders. Two volunteers sit alongside the auctioneer and record the winning bid number for each item. One records on the item's bid sheet and the other on a catalog or separate sheet. In this way, after the auction there can be no dispute about who got each item. Periodically, "runners" carry completed bid sheets to the cashiers, who collate them by bid number.

Never set minimum bids on live-auction items. Leave it up to the auctioneer to decide where the bidding should start, and give him the flexibility to start the bidding low, if need be. You don't ever want to be in the position of having merchandise go unsold.

It's imperative to take care of paperwork *during* the live auction. Says Alana Long: "Everyone will want to check out at the same time at the end of the live auction, and this can 'make or break' your auction. The last thing you want to do is have parents bypass checkout because the line is too long. Then you have to call and track them down, deliver the merchandise, and pick up payment. Instead, you want to have everyone's bill ready when the auction ends."

At Long's school a staff of five to ten volunteers did the accounting throughout the live auction. They periodically got stacks of bid sheets—as the silent auction closed and as items were auctioned during the live auction. They recorded the information from each bid sheet onto the bill of the appropriate high-bidder, so that by the end of the auction each person's bill was complete. (Make out the bill in duplicate using a carbonless receipt so that a copy can be saved for your records.) At Long's school, volunteers even collected the merchandise for each bidder so that checkout went very quickly.

CHECKOUT

Checkout procedures are typically quite straightforward. At the end of the evening guests go to the check-out center, set up at the exit. Let's follow Joe Jones, Bidder Number 220, as he passes through checkout. First he goes to a table and joins the line for people with bid numbers 201–250. He announces his bid number and is handed his bill, which he takes either to the table for people paying by credit card or to the table for those paying by cash or check. Once Joe has paid his bill, a volunteer stamps it "PAID" and hands him a bag or box. Now he's ready to claim his merchandise.

Everything from the silent auction is on display exactly where it was all night, with a volunteer stationed at each table. Goods from the live auction are similarly displayed and staffed. When Joe presents his receipt to the appropriate volunteer, she notes on it that the goods have been claimed, and then Joe takes what he's bought. Schools often set up a separate table where gift certificates can be picked up at the end of the evening. This approach seems to make merchandise claim simpler and has the advantage of keeping all the gift certificates—potentially very valuable—in a secure place.

Committee Responsibilities

You need to get started six months to a year before the auction, depending on how ambitious your plans are. Consider having two overall auction chairs and two chairs-in-training who will take over the next time. Find responsible people to chair the following subcommittees:

> acquisitions
>
> catalog
>
> crew for auction night
>
> decorations
>
> finance
>
> food and beverage
>
> publicity
>
> stage production and lighting

Be careful to match the people to the jobs, trying, for instance, to find someone with a background in graphic arts and/or writing to head the catalog subcommittee. It's particularly important with this difficult fund-raiser that you find competent, organized people who will make the time to devote to their tasks.

Have a meeting of all subcommittee chairs to choose a date, location, and theme for the auction, and decide whom you'd like to use as auctioneer. It helps immensely to have sent parents and teachers a questionnaire asking which subcommittees they'd like to serve on, so that those names can be handed to the appropriate chairs. Give them also, if available, the reports of the people who last chaired their subcommittees.

Clear the date with your principal, book the auctioneer (making sure to get a written agreement, if not a formal contract), reserve your space, and set to work!

ACQUISITIONS

The acquisitions subcommittee has tremendous responsibility, since the success of the entire event depends on the items it collects. The more members it has with varied business and social contacts, the more goods it will acquire. If, for example, a member knows the director of the local performing arts theater or the manager of a baseball team, she'll have a good chance of getting tickets to events and games donated. Even if no one on the committee knows the owner of a business, someone might know an employee or be a regular customer and succeed in getting a donation.

At the initial meeting of the acquisitions subcommittee, the volunteer solicitors need to be trained. The most effective way to elicit donations is to ask merchants in person. "It's much easier to hang up than to walk away," says Toby Schaffer. Although letter-writing campaigns can be successful, they're not nearly as effective as door-to-door solicitation.

A school in Texas did send out letters to merchants telling them that a parent volunteer would be stopping by to solicit a donation. "That way, we volunteers felt more comfortable going in and asking for donations," said Carol David. Being forewarned of a visit also gives a merchant a chance to decide what to donate ahead of time and potentially eliminates the need for a follow-up visit or telephone call.

No volunteer solicitor should go out without a letter of introduction from the PTA. The letter legitimizes his or her request. It should be on letterhead and explain who's having the auction, when it will be held, and what the proceeds will be used for.

Tell volunteers the following: First and foremost, be polite. Explain to the merchant that a donation to the auction is a good way of advertising and that each store's name will be printed in the auction catalog. If you feel that a merchant is going to turn you down, point out that all of the auction guests are potential customers who live nearby. In fact, it is a good idea to suggest at the auction that when guests patronize the stores that donated goods they say, "I remembered your name because of the auction." If approached for future donations, these merchants are likely to remember those comments.

Often merchants ask what an appropriate donation would be. Never give them a dollar figure, and try to get a donation of merchandise instead of a gift certificate. Bidding always stops at the face value of a gift certificate, but people may not know the price of a piece of merchandise and thus may bid far beyond its actual value. It can help to point to an object in the store (never the most expensive item) and say, "This is exactly the kind of thing that's great for us." Often merchants are afraid that you're looking for something that's expensive and they'll be relieved to learn that isn't so. When you select an item in this way, always choose something that's novel, rather than something that most people already have. For instance, at an appliance store, rather than selecting a microwave oven, select an innovative, even if less expensive, gadget—maybe a juicer or a hand-held blender.

Once the volunteer solicitors are trained, assign them merchants whom they are to ask for donations. If you've had an auction before, you should have a master list of stores and what they've donated in the past. Divvy up the list so that each and every one of them is contacted.

You'll probably have the most luck asking local merchants for donations. Kitty Latowicki of Connecticut says that her school PTA was amazed by the response it got. "Ninety percent of local merchants gave us something. We even got a $100 savings bond donated by a local bank. When we went to a neighboring town, though, we only got a couple of donations."

Brainstorm to come up with a list of new businesses. Owners of new stores are receptive to the idea of donating to an auction, because they feel that they can benefit from the resulting publicity. Merchants who sell to the school might contribute to generate goodwill.

Compile a list of local celebrities who might be willing to donate something—a tennis game or lunch, an autographed baseball, book, or photograph. Such items are very much in demand and are often the most popular items at auctions. Even if there aren't any nationally known celebrities living in your town, there are local ones—politicians, corporation presidents, and your own school principal. Ask your state senator or representative to donate a flag flown over the capitol, or to pledge a personal tour of the state capitol. Try to get a golf game with your mayor, a jersey donated by a star football player, or a book autographed by a local author. Once you have a list of celebrities you'd like to approach, assign those individuals to volunteer solicitors on the subcommittee.

Assign a few people the task of soliciting contributions from parents, teachers, corporations, and malls and chain stores. Beyond that, have people specialize in soliciting different categories of goods, such as children's or sports items. The following breakdown works well:

contributions from parents and teachers
contributions from corporations
contributions from malls and chain stores
children's items
pets
gourmet
entertainment
sports
professional services
salons
travel
jewelry and clothing
house and garden

The people in charge of parent and teacher contributions should send a note to parents and teachers letting them know that an auction is being planned and asking them to put the date on their calendars. Ask them how they'd like to help and what they would be willing to donate. Stress that no gift is too small and that two or three families might want to pool resources to donate something. You might give them suggestions of things they could donate: an hour or two of their professional services, a homemade dinner, or a handmade craft. Also ask them if they know any celebrities they could approach for a donation.

The group in charge of corporate, chain store, and mall contributions should decide on overall strategy. Some schools don't solicit from manufacturers. "In our experience, it's easier to get an appliance store to donate a television set than to get one from GE," says Toby Schaffer, three-time chair of a successful school auction. Other schools have had a lot of success with large corporations. As always, a personal contact is very helpful.

Department stores, grocery stores, and even chain discount stores often donate gift certificates in the ten-to-twenty-five-dollar range, and large corporations and shopping malls often donate more if it's to an educational cause. All of these companies typically have committees that meet once a month or so to review these requests, which they require to be in writing. Call each company to find out the appropriate mailing address, and send your request months in advance, making certain to emphasize that the proceeds of the auction will further educational goals and that their gifts are tax-deductible.

Let's move on to other types of donations that are popular at auctions. Here's a description of some of them:

Children's items are an important category since nearly everyone who will attend the auction is a parent.

At the top of the list are *birthday parties,* which can be held at bowling alleys, skating rinks, ice cream parlors, or other popular spots. Unique birthday parties are sensational for the live auction. Ask a dance studio to donate a party—complete with costumes and music—for fifteen children, or get a beauty salon to donate a makeover party for a group of girls. Your own school could donate use of its gym—perhaps with a gym teacher—for an afternoon.

Items made by the children themselves are also popular. At one school, the art teacher supervises the children, who make something to donate to the auction every year. One year, each class made squares for a quilt, and parents sewed them all together. Another year, the children made pottery. In Washington, a public elementary school hosting its first auction asked each classroom to donate a basket with a theme.

Good bets for *games, toys, and books* include: dollhouses, science kits, large stuffed animals, bicycles, kites, games (video and board), collector dolls, gift books (especially autographed ones), computer software, and gift certificates for a certain amount toward an expensive swing set.

Lessons can cover swimming, tennis, dance, gymnastics,

knitting, sewing, or karate. Two or three hours of tutoring or an evening of baby-sitting by a popular teacher also go over very well. All these items are great for the silent auction.

Try to get *a pair of tickets* for free admission to the local children's museum or zoo or to a play, concert, or other performance for children, such as *The Nutcracker.*

Clothing is another popular category. Make sure that there will be people interested in bidding on the particular clothes that you have at your auction. A size-ten boy's suit, for instance, would potentially interest only parents of boys who wear that size. It might be better to have an outfit that could be given as a baby gift or a jacket that could be worn by boys or girls in a two-year age range or a set of headbands or hair bows. Unique items, such as hand-painted clothing and hand-knit baby sweaters are popular, as are gift certificates from shoe stores.

Some stores are willing to donate a gift certificate or exchange an article of clothing for a different size or for store credit. Find out if such alternatives would be acceptable to the stores you're dealing with, and if so, note this information on the acquisitions form and bid sheet.

Pets Some schools auction live pets and accessories for pets. (Show pets only during the cocktail hour so that the pets and audience don't get overly agitated during the live auction!)

Gourmet items are always in demand. The group of people soliciting donations of food should coordinate with the food and beverage subcommittee (discussed on p. 139). It's ideal if the same caterer or grocery store donates both the food served at the cocktail party and the food auctioned off. Ask liquor stores to donate liquor and wine for the auction itself.

The most popular item at an auction is often *a dinner for twelve,* prepared by a caterer and delivered to one's house, sometimes complete with a waiter. Put a dinner like that in the live auction; couples often get together and jointly bid hundreds of dollars for one. Even a homemade lasagna, ethnic, or barbecue dinner, complete with salad and dessert, can be a big hit, particularly if served by the principal or a favorite teacher.

Cocktail or dessert parties for fifty guests are also very popular. Caterers or parents typically make deliveries to the home of the highest bidder. Six teachers or parents are often willing to get together to donate a "dessert a month." Sometimes clubs or restaurants donate parties on their premises, as do parents with beautiful homes or swimming pools. If you have a college or pro team that plays football in town, see if you can get *a tailgate party donated in a motor home.* Sue Hornbeck says, "We have found that a package for *a hot-air balloon flight including a gourmet picnic* is wonderful for birthdays, anniversaries, or gift-giving."

Try to get *a special item of food or drink,* such as a gigantic chocolate bar, a five-foot submarine sandwich, an antique jar filled with gourmet jelly beans, a case or several bottles of fine wine.

Finally, an ever-popular item is *dinner for two (or four)* at a popular restaurant.

Entertainment items generally include *free tickets*—to plays, concerts, tapings of television shows, and movies. You can even auction an entire book of movie tickets. Season passes and expensive or hard-to-get tickets should be in the live auction. One school got four tickets to the taping of an early-morning talk show. It combined them with a limo ride and auctioned the package during the live auction. Other popular items in this category are videotapes and CDs by various artists.

Sports items take in a variety of donations. *Tickets to sporting events* are always popular. Perfect for the live auction: fifty-yard-line tickets to watch your hometown team playing its archrival or field box tickets to a big baseball game. Put other tickets in the silent auction. *Autographed items*—baseballs, footballs, and photos of athletes—are favorites. For the would-be athletes among you, get donations of *sporting equipment* (such as tennis rackets and bicycles), *lessons* (offer golf or tennis lessons with a pro; flying lessons are sensational for the live auction), *health-club memberships, lift tickets* at a ski area, or *tennis court time.*

Donations of professional services run the gamut from an hour or two of work by a plumber, electrician, architect, gardener, interior decorator, or financial planner; to a free cardiac evaluation and stress test performed by a cardiologist; to an exam and cleaning donated by a dentist; to $100 worth of tax preparation by a CPA. The donors can be parents of students in the school or others who work in the community.

Whenever a school auctions the chance to be principal or headmaster for a day, the response is overwhelming!

Donations from salons can be included in both the live and silent auctions. *A complete makeover* or *a full day at a salon* make fun things to bid on as part of a live auction. *Gift certificates* for haircuts, manicures, facials, and makeup lessons belong in the silent auction.

Travel items can include *an exotic trip* (say, a trip to Hawaii for two, including airfare and hotel) or *a day on someone's boat* or *use of a lakeside cottage or seaside duplex* for a weekend after Labor Day. Hotels and country inns sometimes donate *weekend getaway packages,* and travel agents may offer *airline or cruise tickets.*

Be sure to include **jewelry and clothing.** All sorts of jewelry do well at an auction. In terms of clothing, depending on season and climate, you might do well with sweaters, jackets, coats, and unique items.

Artwork, crystal, china, clocks, lamps, appliances, picture frames, trays, books, vases, plants and silk flower arrangements all fall within the category of **house and garden items.** If someone donates an original piece of art, put it in the live auction. You might be able to get a florist to supply a flower arrangement a month. That would work well in the live auction as well. Try to get a photographer to provide a free family portrait.

KEEPING TRACK OF ACQUISITIONS

Sometimes merchants will hand over their donations on the spot, and sometimes the solicitor or a separate subcommittee will have to go back and pick them up later. In either case, information about the donation must be put in the school's records, and the merchant must be given a receipt for his records. This can be done in several ways, but it's easiest if you use a four-part acquisition form printed on NCR paper. Record on it:

> item acquisition number
> individual donor's or company's name as it should appear
> in the catalog

donor's name (actual contact person) and address for
thank-you letter

complete description of the item

estimated value of the item

when it's to be picked up and by whom

where it's being stored

solicitor's name

donor's signature

purchaser's bid number

With a four-part form, one copy can be given to the donor
as a receipt; one can go to the catalog subcommittee; the
solicitor can keep one for her own records in case there are any
questions and so that she'll know when to pick up the item;
and one will become a receipt for the purchaser. (Some auctioneers sell these preprinted forms.)

Instead of a four-part form, you can simply record the
same information on a comprehensive "merchandise sheet"
and give a separate receipt to the donor.

As soon as you pick up an item, label it with its acquisition
number and mark on its acquisitions form where it's being
stored—in a central location in the school or in someone's
basement, for instance. All records should, of course, be cross-
referenced. Merchants donating gift certificates probably already have them on hand. Most parents donating services don't
have gift certificates, however, so you need to prepare some
blank certificates.

Some schools write thank-you letters as they receive each
item, and others wait until the very end or do them in a few
batches. Whatever the time frame, as soon as the thank-you
goes out, put a check mark on the acquisitions form indicating
that an acknowledgment has been sent. (Some schools use a
five-part acquisitions form, so that a thank-you team can have
one copy for its use.)

CATALOG

This subcommittee is responsible for writing, designing, and
producing the auction catalog and invitations.

If the auction has a theme, it should be incorporated into

the invitations and catalog, in terms of both text and illustrations. For example, a school that used a safari theme put a drawing of a tiger's head on the cover of its catalog, called "Treasures of the Wild."

You can create the invitations and catalog on a personal computer and then either copy them or have them printed professionally. Early on, check into the cost of professional printing. If you can get a printer to donate his or her time and to charge only for materials, the cost might be within reach. (You'll save a lot of expense if you deliver your copy to the printer camera-ready.)

The invitations, which go to all the school parents and teachers, need not be fancy, but you'll want to include response cards or a tear-off reservation form so that you'll get a head count and be able to distribute catalogs in advance of the auction. (Everybody who attends the auction needs to get a copy of the catalog.) Don't be surprised if you get most of your reservations three or four days before the deadline.

The catalog should list the silent auction categories and closing times, each item to be auctioned, and the name of every donor. It must also include thank-yous to all the subcommittee heads and volunteers who worked on the auction and state the rules of both the live and silent auctions. Many schools sell advertising space in the back of the catalog. If you choose to do so, form a separate team within either the acquisitions or catalog subcommittee to solicit ads. (See Chapter 10.)

The following procedure for *assembling the catalog* is highly recommended. As the acquisitions subcommittee collects goods, it forwards one copy of each acquisition form to the catalog subcommittee. The catalog subcommittee then enters the data into its computer, filing each donation by acquisition number and category—gourmet, travel, children's, and so on. When the subcommittee sits down to write the copy for the catalog, the information is then readily available.

The catalog subcommittee will have to decide which items to put in the silent auction and which in the live, which items to package together, and then assign appropriate catalog numbers to the items.

A professional auctioneer will tell you how many items he

or she can auction in the two or two and a half hours available for the live auction. A school principal or a parent who's acting as an auctioneer for the first time should plan on auctioning no more than forty items in the live auction. Whether you're going to auction forty or ninety items live, however, choose the most desirable items for the live auction, and put everything else in the silent auction. (A professional auctioneer will help you make these choices.) Hundreds of items should wind up in the silent auction if the acquisitions subcommittee has done a good job.

As a general rule, you're likely to make more money if you auction items separately rather than packaging them together. Some packages do make sense, however. Beatty and Kirkpatrick suggest putting together a package of school supplies (globe, bookends, and encyclopedia or dictionary) or a package of painting supplies (easel, paints, paper, and smock). One school put together a humorous package of a dozen donuts and two free dental cleanings. As a general guideline, don't auction as a separate item anything worth less than $10. Any excess of inexpensive items need not be consolidated into packages; the items can be given away as door prizes or used as duck pond prizes (described on p. 141).

Once the catalog subcommittee has put together packages and allocated goods to the live or silent auction, it assigns catalog numbers to them, giving a great deal of thought to the order in which the goods should be auctioned at the live auction (see discussion on pp. 124–26).

The catalog should describe each item that will be raffled off and provide the name of the donor alongside. Then it should list and highlight the items that will be in the live auction. (Describe each item first in a cute or funny way and then in a concise, descriptive way, including the donor's name.) Items that will be in the silent auction should be listed last; arrange them by category (such as children's or home and garden), with each category heading playing on the auction's theme. Each item in the catalog must be numbered and listed in numerical order. The letter prefix or first digits of each item's number indicate its category—L001 being the first item to be auctioned live, for instance, and C001 the first item in the children's category of the silent auction. (Sample pages modeled on a public school's auction catalog appear at the end of the chapter.)

Have the catalogs ready to be distributed two weeks before the auction. Any donations received after the catalog goes to print can be listed in an addendum inserted in the catalogs.

As soon as the catalog subcommittee has decided what will go in the silent auction, a pricing team can begin its work. The latter needs to set minimum bids and raises for each item in the silent auction and then fill out bid sheets for every item—silent and live.

PUBLICITY

This subcommittee is responsible for sending fliers to teachers and parents, advertising, and generating community publicity. Kitty Latowicki explains what her publicity subcommittee did: "We put ads in the local newspaper, and they also printed (for free) a photograph of the auction committee, the auctioneers, and principal, along with a couple of the items to be auctioned. We also got free advertising by writing a letter to the editor of the paper about the event and why we were having it."

DECORATIONS

This subcommittee doesn't need to get going in full gear as early as the others, but it should recruit artistic members and begin thinking about how to decorate around the theme. Try to find a florist, nursery, or balloon company to donate centerpieces, and then auction them off. (Have people sitting at each table write their bids on little pieces of paper that have been distributed, and sell the centerpieces to the highest bidders.)

The decorations subcommittee is responsible not only for decorations but also for making or buying the paddles that will be used at the live auction itself. "We make our own paddles," says Sue Hornbeck. "They look like cardboard stop signs on tongue depressors." Always make sure that the paddles have huge, bold numbers on front and back, since it's essential that the auctioneer be able to read the numbers. Decorate the paddles in keeping with the auction's theme. For an Oriental theme, you might make paddles that look like fans, for instance. If it's not feasible to make paddles, buy them from a professional auctioneer, or simply write each person's bidding number on the back of his or her catalog.

FOOD AND BEVERAGE

Working alongside the acquisitions subcommittee, this subcommittee asks parents, teachers, and businesses for donations of food and drink as well as paper goods, coffeepots, punch bowls, and whatever other supplies are needed. It needs to arrange for waiters for the night of the auction. High school students or alumni can work well in this capacity and free parents to bid in the auction. (Make sure no one underage serves alcohol, however.)

CREW FOR AUCTION NIGHT

This subcommittee must recruit volunteers to set up, clean up, staff the silent auction tables, record winning bids during the live auction, display the live auction goods, and act as runners, spotters, and security people. Always ask a few people to be "floaters." Just setting up the auction is an enormous undertaking, which ideally can be done the day before the event, if security is adequate. Consider hiring an off-duty police officer to guard the room after everything is set up, particularly if your auction will not be held at school.

A group of artistic or dramatic parents can work out how they'll display the goods during the live auction. Line up people to put together skits or a slide show and to write up descriptions of each good on index cards for the auctioneer's use. Some of the live auction items can be displayed on a stage during the silent auction.

FINANCE

Responsibilities of the finance subcommittee are spelled out earlier in this chapter. Insist that all goods be paid for the night of the auction—by cash, check, or credit card. Check with banks to get the best rates for credit cards and to learn how to take them. Make sure that your credit card table is stationed by a telephone. Make your bank deposit the night of the auction.

Extras

Schools that are old hands at running auctions add extra flourishes, such as raffles or games for the parents. One year, in keeping with a carnival theme, a school that had traditionally hosted a black-tie auction decided to make the dress informal and offer carnival games for parents during the silent auction. The innovations were such a success that the committee decided to make the games a permanent feature of their auction. When another school chose a Monte Carlo theme for its pre-auction party, parents played roulette and blackjack, and fireworks went off at midnight.

RAFFLES

Even if your school is trying an auction for the first time, have a raffle. (Before you do so, though, check to make sure that it's legal in your state.) Sell raffle tickets both in the weeks before the auction and during the silent auction, and announce the winners during the live auction.

Another option is to raffle off several items at the same time. On one table, display the five or ten items that you've decided to raffle in this way. These items—such as baskets full of goodies or dinner for two at a nice restaurant—should be chosen for their wide appeal. One school purchased a dollhouse kit at cost through a museum store, and a father assembled it. The dollhouse brought in more than $1,000 when it was raffled at the school's auction. If yours is a private school, raffle off a year's free tuition. Even if you charge a lot per ticket, nearly every parent and grandparent will buy one.

BALLOONS

Sell balloons for $10 to $25 each. Either attached to the string or inside the balloon put a numbered card that the purchaser can redeem for a prize. Include several very nice prizes. One person stationed at a table can both sell the balloons and distribute the prizes (which are stored underneath the table), or one person can roam around (with a hat pin) selling balloons and another can be stationed at the prize table. Instead of giving away material prizes, you can put bills or small gift certificates into the balloons. (Helium balloons, by the way, pose a threat to the environment.)

TREASURE CHEST

Decorate a treasure chest and sell inexpensive tickets for it. At the end of the evening, draw five or ten tickets. (This is a good way to induce people to stay until the end of the auction.) The holders of the winning tickets each get a real key. The person whose key actually opens the chest wins the treasure inside.

DUCK POND

Set up a little wading pool filled with rubber duckies. Paint stars on the undersides of some of the ducks, and sell chances to go fishing in the pond. Anyone who catches one of the winning ducks gets a nicely wrapped gift. Alternatively, paint numbers on the ducks, with the numbers corresponding to different gifts.

Auctions with Merchandise Themes

The biggest money-raisers are almost always auctions of the sort just described—those of general-purpose merchandise. If you like the idea of an auction but are afraid of the amount of work entailed, consider having just a silent auction or an auction of only a specialized type of merchandise. The amount of money that you raise will naturally depend on the quality and quantity of goods that you gather. Schools have auctioned off cakes, items donated by celebrities or faculty, and artwork donated by private owners and by galleries.

ART AUCTIONS

The potential for raising large sums isn't nearly as great with an art auction as with a full-fledged auction, but an art auction is easy to run. Soliciting, collecting, and cataloging merchandise constitutes 90 percent of the effort associated with a full-fledged auction, and with an art auction the art gallery takes care of all that.

The gallery typically selects the work to be auctioned, delivers it to the site of the auction, and furnishes an auctioneer. What's left to the school, then, is advertising, arranging for refreshments and decorations, helping set up the artwork, and taking money. (Note that some galleries require the school to insure the artwork against theft and damage.) The school keeps an agreed-upon percentage of the proceeds (usually 10 to 20 percent, depending on the volume of sales).

Most art auctions are held in the evening. During the first hour, people preview the artwork, which is on display around the room. Generally, finger food and cocktails are served during this time, and the auctioneer is available to answer questions about individual pieces.

The auction itself lasts about two and a half hours. Volunteer "runners" carry the pieces one by one to the front of the room, where they're displayed on an easel. The auctioneer begins the bidding at a prespecified minimum bid and rapidly auctions off about 200 pieces, putting in the unsold pile anything that doesn't sell after a few quick tries.

At the end of the auction, the gallery takes back any unsold merchandise, and the school volunteers need only clean up the room and do the bookkeeping.

✳   ✳   ✳

SILENT AUCTION RULES

1. Bidding will close by section.

2. Winners will be posted as soon as possible after each section is closed.

3. You do not have to be present to win. Payment and pickup must occur within seven days from the close of the auction or the next bidder will be entitled to the item.

4. Each bid MUST have name, auction number, and bid legibly printed.

5. You may bid as often as you like on each item.

6. If the proper raise in price has not been adhered to, the previous bidder may be entitled to the item.

7. Cash or checks will be accepted. Checks may be made out to the Lincoln School PTA.

8. ALL SALES ARE FINAL.

9. Cash or checks only. No Fun Fair tickets, please.

Catalog quantities are limited. Please bring your copy of this catalog with you to the auction. Thank you.

SILENT AUCTION CATEGORIES AND CLOSING TIMES

100
"Bon Appetit"
Food
8:15 P.M.

200
"Billboard"
Entertainment
8:15 P.M.

300
"Yellow Pages"
Services
8:30 P.M.

400
"Sports Illustrated"
Sports and Leisure
8:30 P.M.

500
"Better Homes & Gardens"
House and Garden
8:45 P.M.

600
"Cosmopolitan"
Personal His and Hers
8:45 P.M.

700
"Potpourri"
Miscellaneous
9:00 P.M.

"SPORTS ILLUSTRATED"
Sports and Leisure

401—Super Field Trip
A trail ride on a Tennessee Walker to Great Falls Park.

(donor's name)

402—Adventures in Mask Making
A three-session mask-making and design class for two students (aged five and up—adults welcome).

(donor's name)

403—What's Your Racket?
One Prince International 110 4⅜" tennis racket.

(donor's name)

404—Can't Wait Till August!
One campership for the fourth session (from _____ to_____) at _____ School's Camp _____

(donor's name)

405—Shape Up for Bathing Suit Season
Five aerobics classes.

(donor's name)

406—Happy Camper
One-week session of Elementary Day Camp (9:00 A.M.–3:00 P.M.) from _____ to_____ , excluding Red Cross swimming lesson. Pre-enroll two weeks prior to session.

(donor's name)

407—Great Great Falls Pastime
Eight group English-style horseback riding lessons of fifty minutes each. Requires proper attire and safety equipment. Good between _____ and _____ .

(donor's name)

408—Needlecraft, the Restful Sport
One needlecraft pillow kit.

(donor's name)

409—For Budding Ballerinas
Six ballet lessons.

(donor's name)

410—Free Driving
Three days of weekend car rental, excluding specialty models.

(donor's name)

411—Dynomites Party with Paula
One hour of birthday party entertainment for fifteen children.

(donor's name)

412—Fun in the Sun with Discovery Toys
Three of Discovery Toys' most popular toys: Critter Catcher, Give It a Whirl, and Sun Shots.

(donor's name)

413—If Tennis Is Your Racket . . .
Enjoy . . . with this Prince DB 110 model.

(donor's name)

414—Make Some Friends
Model kits for five dinosaurs, including a Dinosaur Dictionary and wall poster.

(donor's name)

415—Keeping Small Hands Busy
One basket-weaving set.

(donor's name)

BID SHEET

Item _____

_____

Donated By _____

_____

Minimum Raise: $_____

Minimum Bid: $_____

Bid Number   Amount of Bid

1. _____

2. _____

3. _____

4. _____

5. _____

6. _____

7. _____

8. _____

9. _____

10. _____

11. _____

12. _____

13. _____

14. _____

15. _____

16. _____

17. _____

18. _____

19. _____

20. _____

CHAPTER SEVEN

FUN FAIRS I: GREAT IDEAS

WHAT COULD BE BETTER THAN A FUN FAIR TO BUILD SCHOOL spirit, give children a wonderful day, and raise funds for the school at the same time? As Jennifer Harris of Dallas says: "Our school has a Halloween carnival that really gets the community involved. I think it's great, because the product you're selling is 'fun,' and the kids benefit by the money you make, too."

Maybe your school has never had a fun fair and you're afraid to try one because you just don't know how to get started or you're afraid of the amount of work entailed. In this chapter I show you how to run a successful fun fair by delegating responsibility to make the job manageable. You can start out on a small scale the first year and add activities as you gain experience. Read on to learn the ropes from parents who've been running fun fairs for years. If your school already has an annual fun fair, but you want to spruce it up with some new activities, you're sure to find a few ideas here that you can tailor to your own school event.

WHAT IS A FUN FAIR?

A fun fair is a carnival full of exciting activities for the whole family. Children buy tickets, usually for a nominal price, which entitle them to play games and make crafts at booths operated or supervised by parents. Ring tosses, dart throws, fishing games, face painting, and beanbag tosses are standard features at just about every fun fair. Most schools hold their fairs for several hours on a Saturday or Sunday and sell hot dogs, pizza, popcorn, and ice cream. Beyond that, the ingenuity of people shows itself in every fun fair. Each seems to feature unique activities and has its own character.

Along with the games and crafts, schools create a carnival atmosphere at their fun fairs by having other activities, such as:

silent auctions

sales of plants, crafts, used books and toys, or baked goods

performances

competitions for children and parents

dunking machines or moon walks

pony or donkey rides

animal displays and petting zoos

HOW MUCH MONEY CAN YOU EXPECT TO MAKE?

The profit to be made from a fun fair can range from a minimal amount to several thousand dollars. An elementary school in McLean, Virginia, raises $10,000 to $12,000 annually from its fun fair. Tickets cost 20 cents each (six for a dollar if purchased in advance), with most activities requiring between one and four tickets each. Many schools shoot to break even on their fun fairs or make only a nominal sum, viewing them more as providing a service for the school community than as an opportunity to raise funds. Sensitive to the fact that families may be unable to afford much per ticket, they charge only a token amount—usually twenty-five cents per activity.

Even when ticket prices are kept low, however, a school can still make a few thousand dollars from a fun fair that offers lots of sales and activities simultaneously, so that there's something for everyone. A 650-student school in New Jersey raises about $6,500 from its Mayfair every year, even though it charges only twenty-five cents per game.

WHEN AND WHERE SHOULD YOU HAVE YOUR FUN FAIR?

Fun fairs can be held at any time of year, but most take place in the fall or spring. October fairs with a harvest or Halloween theme are popular. Judy Dannes says that her elementary school in Schenectady, New York, moved its fair from the spring to the fall to welcome new families to the school. The PTO sends invitations to its "Fall Frolic" to all new families, and the principal gives them free tickets. Using a Halloween theme makes it easy to come up with creative activities (described on pp. 151–53).

Fun fairs that are celebrations of springtime are also very popular and allow plenty of time during the school year for planning and preparation. These fun fairs are usually held outdoors, often in conjunction with a plant sale. Winter carnivals help beat winter doldrums, although in harsh climates where snow would mean a cancellation, fun fairs aren't usually scheduled in the winter.

What Time During the Week Is Best?

Have your fun fair on a Saturday or Sunday for about five hours, staying open long enough so that people with other commitments are able to attend. Any longer than about five hours, though, and you'll have trouble getting enough volunteers. Deborah Kahn, cochair of a large fun fair in Virginia, says that a core group of parents spends all day at their fair—from 9:00 A.M. to 5:00 P.M.—even though official opening hours are 10:00 to 3:00, and they set up the day before.

Should the Fair Be Indoors or Out?

If you don't want to take any chances with the weather, have the fair indoors—maybe with a few activities outdoors, weather permitting. A Virginia school has its fair indoors in March every year, with one or two rented activities, such as a moon bounce, outdoors if the weather is nice. The contract with the company that provides the moon bounce specifies that the school won't have to pay anything if the weather is inclement and it chooses not to rent the moon bounce. Alternatively, you could plan to set up the moon bounce indoors if it rained. Rain or shine, many schools find it to be one of the biggest money-makers.

An indoor fair has the advantage of eliminating a lot of worry and allowing you to easily draw up a floor plan of where various activities will be. One school distributes a floor plan to everyone attending its fair. (See sample floor plan at the end of the chapter.) On the other hand, an indoor fair can generate a terrible mess, and the exciting atmosphere of an outdoor fair is hard to replicate indoors. Whether your fair is indoors or out, people must have access to toilet facilities.

If you plan an outdoor fair, have a contingency plan drawn up in case of rain. Either schedule a rain date for the following day and devise a plan to notify everyone of the change, or hold the fair indoors, making sure the location of each activity has been selected in advance. Kathleen Bennett says that one year the Mayfair had to be moved indoors a few hours before it was scheduled to begin. Had the fair committee not had a detailed plan drawn up, they never would have been able to pull it off.

HOW MANY VOLUNTEERS WILL BE NEEDED?

A full-fledged fun fair requires many volunteers. At one school's fair, sixty volunteers were able to staff a five-hour-long fair that included lots of different activities: six games, five craft activities, a café, a sale of used books and toys, a plant sale, cupcake decorating, raffles with hourly drawings, a dozen vendors, moon bounce, ball crawl (a large room filled knee-deep with soft balls the size of tennis balls in which kids play barefoot), pony rides, and performances throughout the day.

If this is your school's first fun fair, plan for fewer activities and volunteers. Count on a minimum of two volunteers per shift for each game or craft, with three or four shifts over the course of the day. Some volunteers should be unassigned prior to the fair and used where needed that day.

Plan to have two parents cochair the fair, and have them delegate authority to people on the fair committee. For step-by-step planning, see Chapter 8.

SHOULD YOU DO IT ALL OR WORK THROUGH A SUPPLIER?

By making all the games, you can save them from year to year and even share them with neighboring schools. By working through a supplier, you can simply select the games and prizes and let the company do the rest. The day before the fair, the company delivers the games and prizes and sets up the games where you'd like them. It charges a rental fee for each game as well as retail prices for the prizes that are used; generally speaking, unopened boxes of prizes can be returned. The evening of the fair or the next day, the company picks up the games and unused prizes.

The big advantage of using a company is that it eliminates the tasks of designing the games and ordering prizes. The obvious drawback is that it's a more expensive alternative. The PTA at one school had always rented the twelve to fourteen games at its fun fair every year. One year, it saved nearly $1,000 by making six games and renting only eight.

WHAT KIND OF PRIZES SHOULD BE AWARDED?

At each game, you can either award prizes or give children tokens or tickets that they accumulate and redeem for a prize of their choosing at a central prize booth. Children—especially young ones—love to get prizes at each game, and some schools make sure that everybody "wins" each time they play a game. Of course, this can be expensive unless the prizes are just trinkets such as plastic rings that might not have much lasting value. Awarding prizes at a central location requires a few more volunteers and some additional planning and organization but can leave the children with more lasting mementos of the day. If you choose to have a central prize booth, allow the children to buy prizes with cash as well as with tokens.

Paula Swain of Virginia, who was in charge of prizes and games at a large fun fair one year, confirms that awarding prizes on the spot to the little children every time they play a game is good psychology. For older children, she thinks it works better to award prizes at a central prize booth. Consider awarding prizes on the spot at the games for little children and at a central spot for the other games. As consolation prizes, hand out individually wrapped candies. (Why not ask parents to donate these?)

Most schools order their prizes in bulk and offer a merry (and inexpensive) assortment of bouncing balls, yo-yos, pencils, erasers, hair clips, shoelaces, magic tricks, and plastic jewelry.

SHOULD YOUR FAIR HAVE A THEME?

If your school is having its very first fun fair, using a theme might make planning too complicated—unless you use the Fall harvest/Halloween theme described below. If your school already has a fun fair every year, incorporating a new theme might be just the way to give it some pizzazz.

One year, Sharon Gordon, cochair of the fun fair at a Virginia school, came up with the idea of using a "train" theme. The fun fair guide, "All Aboard," pictured a train on the cover. All literature about the fair that went home to families was done in red—announcing the arrival of the Fun Fair Express. The PTO sponsored a poster contest. One child made an engine, one made a caboose, and the other children's posters each featured one of the cars in between. The PTO decorated the school's hallways with the poster-train, rented an electric, trackless train, and offered rides the day of the fair.

One school used a clown motif for its fair for several years. The clown was pictured on all posters and notices about the fair, and a real clown appeared at the fair.

Fall Harvest/Halloween Theme

A school in upstate New York has its Fall Frolic in the middle of October, with activities centered on a harvest theme. The PTO sponsors a contest to see which classroom can make the best scarecrow, with prizes for funniest, scariest, most like an animal, and so forth. A few weeks beforehand, the PTO supplies each class with some basic materials—a wooden cross and plastic garbage bags for stuffing. By the day of the fair, the scarecrows are on display decorating the schoolyard. Local celebrities (including the school principal, a television weather reporter, and a state senator) judge the scarecrow contest the day of the fair. One year, the grand prize for the younger children (in kindergarten through second grade) went to a scarecrow that looked like the Cat in the Hat, a character in a Dr. Seuss story, and that for the older children (in the third through fifth grades) went to the Wolf in Granny's Clothing, borrowing from "Little Red Riding Hood." The winning classes got pizza parties.

The PTO sells cider and donuts and has a contest for the best-tasting pumpkin pie. Pumpkins are sold on consignment from a farmer who agrees to take back those that don't sell, and a contest is held to see who can paint the best face on a pumpkin. A mother dresses as a witch, and a father dresses as the Great Pumpkin and hands out trinkets to the children. (The entire schedule of activities for this Fall Frolic appears at the end of the chapter.)

A school in Wellesley, Massachusetts, has a fun fair right before Halloween. The organizers set up a white picket fence with a black cat perched on top. Children take turns throwing balls at the cat to try to knock it over. At another booth, they throw hoops and attempt to hook a skeleton. There's a contest to see who comes closest to guessing the number of pieces of candy corn in a bowl.

A haunted house is featured in the school hallway. A parent dresses as Frankenstein's monster and leads the little children through, where they're scared by high school students in costume who jump out at them, a witch stirring a steaming caldron full of dry ice, and a "coffin" with a person in it.

Gay Lee Einstein says of her school's annual haunted house in Virginia: "I dressed as a witch and held out a bowl full of stewed prunes, asking children if they wanted to touch some eyeballs. We decorated with sheets and had a mannequin in a coffin atop a draped table. A parent hid underneath this table and waved a hand back and forth from the coffin. People in costumes walked around moaning, the scariest being the Hunchback of Notre Dame."

Jennifer Harris talks about the Halloween fun fair at her children's school in Texas: "The best part was the spook house, which we called the 'Mad Scientist's Laboratory.' It was in the basement, which most kids didn't even know about, and was already perfectly creepy! We made sure it was very safe and more clever than really scary, because I have a real dislike of those gross, gory haunted houses you find these days."

Jan Smith reports that for their haunted house at a school near St. Louis, parents created separate rooms using black plastic Visqueen as dividers. With fluorescent paint, they created scary scenes on the plastic, which they lit up with black lights to give everything an eerie glow.

At the fall festival at a school in Maryland, parents set up a pumpkin patch. Using about five bales of hay, they created an obstacle course, spreading some of the bales and leaving some intact. They scattered around sixty pounds' worth of mini-pumpkins, and for a ticket a child could go through and find a pumpkin to take home. For another ticket, a parent could watch through a peephole in the back. In a separate room they made butter and cider.

Some schools encourage children to attend in costume, and others sell used costumes at their fun fairs. At an elementary school in Dallas, everyone attends the "Haunted Hollow" in costume, and there is a costume contest. A fortune-teller, a pickpocket witch, and lots of carnival-type games add a Halloween twist. In "spider toss," kids toss a big rubber spider with curved wire legs and try to hook it on a cargo net. At "pumpkin bounce" kids try to shoot orange basketballs painted with jack-o-lantern faces into trash cans.

WHAT ACTIVITIES ARE POPULAR?

Every fun fair has its own unique collection of activities. Here is a full complement of ideas from which to choose.

Crafts

Set up tables where children can make crafts. The possibilities are endless. You'll find some good ideas in this section, and most libraries have useful books of craft ideas. Fall fun fairs afford the perfect opportunity for children to make simple things that they can give as holiday gifts.

MACARONI NECKLACES

At one school, parents are asked to donate macaroni that they've dyed different colors, and children make necklaces at the fun fair. The kids string the macaroni on twenty-inch lengths of tape-wrapped wire (bought in rolls from a florist and cut to size). "We used picture wire in the past, but kids kept getting poked by it. This works much better," says Kathleen Bennett. When each necklace is strung, a parent knots it in the back.

DECORATIVE BONNETS OR PICTURES

Gather feathers, sequins, buttons, scraps of fabric and rickrack, silk flowers, colored glue, and glitter, and have children decorate a paper plate to create a bonnet. Or instead of bonnets, have children create decorative pictures using Styrofoam meat trays the parents have collected.

PLAY-DOH

As every parent knows, young children like nothing better than to mold something out of Play-Doh. Ask parents to donate homemade modeling dough, and set up a place where children can play with it. After the fair, give the leftovers to the kindergarten teachers.

PAPER AIRPLANES

A parent at one school teaches children how to make their own paper airplanes. Needless to say, this one event has really taken off!

BUTTONS OR MAGNETS

You can buy or borrow a machine to make buttons or magnets, and this makes another great activity. (A magnet machine costs about $70, for example, and can be used year after year.) At a Virginia school, fair organizers suggest that children bring in a photograph or picture from home to make into a magnet. They also use drawings of popular figures that children can color for their magnets. Four volunteers work each shift, one at each magnet machine.

SWIRL ART/FINGER PAINTING/"MESSY ART"

Set up a table where children can freely do messy artwork that parents often won't permit at home. The kids can make designs with finger paints, a swirl-art kit, or shaving cream.

Games

LOLLIPOP TREE/BEAR/STAR/CLOWN

The lollipop tree is a sort of lottery where everyone goes away with at least a lollipop. Lollipops are stuck into a Styrofoam cone or pegboard and arranged to look like a tree, bear, star, or clown. The sticks of some of the lollipops are marked at the tip, and the child who gets one of those gets a prize in addition to the lollipop. (The same can be done with pencils instead of lollipops.) "Little children love this one," says Deborah Kahn of Virginia.

RING TOSS

There are many variations on this old theme. Children throw rings at milk bottles, bunny ears, antlers, or anything else you can think of.

At one school, the older children love "poster toss," where ringing a poster entitles them to take it home. The posters are on three-foot dowels fitted onto a plywood board that a father made several years ago. Every year, the PTO writes to *Sports Illustrated* asking for a donation of outdated sports posters.

Jo Cirelli of Lincoln Park, New Jersey, says that at her school the PTA uses one-liter bottles of soda and cans of Pringle's potato chips for the ring toss. Kids get to take home anything that they ring.

FISHING

The basic idea is to erect a barrier—with a sheet or a cardboard wall—and have each child throw a fishing rod over the top. Behind, someone attaches a little prize to the fishing rod and sends it back over. The fishing rod is simply a pole—broom handle or bamboo pole—with a string attached. At the end of the string is a clothespin, making it easy to attach trinkets to the pole. At one school, the prize is a biscuit baked in the shape of a fish.

BASKETBALL

Give children a certain number of tries to make a basket. For young children, you can set up a miniature (or oversized) basketball hoop placed at little-people height.

PROSPECTING FOR GOLD OR "MAGIC" PENNIES

Fill a plastic wading pool with sand, and hide pennies in it. Give children a chance to fill a scoop with sand and sift through it to find pennies. The young prospectors can also dip their pennies in a solution of vinegar, which "magically" makes them shine.

WIN A GOLDFISH

Have children toss Ping-Pong balls toward a tank. Anyone who gets one in takes home a goldfish. One school bought 200 goldfish for its fun fair and gave them all away. Marcia DeOteris gives the following advice: "As you can imagine, this is a very popular activity. Make sure you give it lots of room and a place to store the goldfish that children win, each in a plastic bag of water labeled with the winner's name, ready to be reclaimed when it's time to go home."

HOCKEY/SOCCER

Position a volunteer goalie in front of a net. Give each child several chances to try to score a goal.

FOOTBALL

Hang a tire on a rope suspended from a basketball hoop. Let children try to throw a football through the tire. Or have children throw wet sponges through toilet bowl seats! This one guarantees lots of giggles.

BOWLING

Try to get used bowling pins from a bowling alley. Failing that, use milk cartons. Lynn Fornadel of Delaware suggests using two pieces of plywood measuring four feet by eight feet to make an alley.

PEANUT OR BEANBAG TOSS

Paint the face of an elephant on plywood, and give it a cone-shaped nose. Let children toss peanuts into the elephant's nose. Lynn Fornadel says young children love this game. Joyce Richardson of Seattle, Washington, notes that at her school's fair children toss beanbags at a plywood clown made by a parent. The clown is painted and has an open mouth and belly with a hole cut in it.

MAKE A FUNNY FACE

Paint a picture of a silly-looking, child-sized person on a sheet of plywood and cut out a hole where the face would be. Let children stick their faces in the hole for a good laugh.

OBSTACLE COURSE

Arrange large cardboard boxes to make tunnels for children to crawl through. Barbara Corner says that this game was a big hit at her school in Birmingham, Alabama.

TIN CAN ALLEY

Set up three cans covered with paper of different colors. Arrange them in a pyramid on a table or individually on the floor. Have children try to knock them down with a ball or beanbag.

You can award different points to the different cans so that, for instance, knocking down the red can would be worth more points than toppling the blue can.

DARTS

Set up a dart game using balloons and real darts, or, to be safer, Velcro darts.

DINOSAUR ROCK

This game is a favorite at a Virginia school. Parents save the egg-shaped cartons from pantyhose and fill each carton with a trinket related to dinosaurs—a pencil, eraser, or dinosaur figurine. A huge box is decorated to look like a cave and then filled with Styrofoam peanuts, scattered with dinosaur "eggs" throughout. Children search to unearth a dinosaur egg of their own. The fair organizers devote an entire classroom to the dinosaur rock, decorating the room with inflatable dinosaurs, drawings, and posters of dinosaurs.

LUCKY DUCKY

Buy or borrow a tiny kiddie swimming pool, and fill it with water. Buy seven weighted ducks and attach numbers to their undersides. Buy seven different types of prizes, and line them up behind the pool, giving each type of prize a different number. A child who catches a duck that has a number five underneath wins one of the number-five prizes.

SWING BALL

Set up three bowling pins on the floor. Attach one end of a rope to a basketball hoop, and tie a baseball to the other end. Have a child stand back with the rope pulled taut, so that the child, the bowling pins, and the basketball hoop form a triangle. The child throws the ball beyond the pins and scores points by knocking the pins over as the ball makes its way back.

MINIATURE GOLF

The McLean, Virginia, school tried a short golf course (dubbed "putt-putt golf") one year, but fair organizers discontinued it because it was too slow-moving and created long lines. On the other hand, an elementary school in Reston, Virginia, had good luck setting up a hole-in-one course with just one hole and giving children a few tries to score.

WHOSE FEET?

Have several teachers stand behind a curtain with only their bare feet showing. Then have kids try to identify whose feet they are.

Special Activities and Characters

DOLL HOSPITAL

One school sets up a "doll hospital," where adults are stationed with needle and thread, ready to try to mend any doll or stuffed animal for the price of a ticket. Make sure to let children know in advance about the doll hospital, so they can bring in their sick dolls.

"MASH" TENT

The PTA at a school in Raleigh, North Carolina, sets up a "MASH" tent at its fun fair. Off-duty nurses make up children to look as if they've been extras in Hollywood war movies—giving the young actors "bloody" bandages, cuts, bruises, and burns. The kids love it.

FACE PAINTING

Another of the children's favorites, face painting, is easy to do. Recruit parents with some artistic talent. Make sure that you have enough parents on duty to avoid long lines. (At a New Jersey school, six parents paint faces at each shift.) Display designs so children can select one while waiting in line. Use acrylic paints in small paint pots. (Make sure that the paints are safe to apply to faces.) Kathleen Bennett says that her school had to charge more for face painting than for the other activities, because the paints are expensive, and the school lost money when charging only twenty-five cents for it. However, this is one activity that warrants a higher price tag.

BEAUTY SALON

Jo Cirelli says, "The biggest hit at our fair was a beauty salon set up by a PTA mom who made French braids and did manicures."

PHOTO STOP

At a school in McLean, Virginia, children love to have their photographs taken standing next to their favorite movie stars. The PTO asks local video stores for stand-up advertising billboards and movie posters. Children pay $2 to pose next to a billboard and have their picture taken with a Polaroid camera; they also have a chance to win one of the posters, which are raffled off throughout the day.

CAKEWALK

Even adults love a good cakewalk. The floor is marked with twenty to twenty-five numbered spots in a big circle, each one large enough for a person to stand on. At the beginning of the cakewalk, each person stands on a number. When the music starts, they walk around in a circle, and when the music ends, each one steps onto the nearest number. The caller draws a number, and the person standing on that number gets to take home the donated cake of his or her choosing.

Marcia DeOteris offers this tip: "It's really important to have a loud caller to draw attention to the cakewalk. Otherwise, kids just pass it by."

At one school, sixth-graders are asked to donate cakes, and the class that brings in the most cakes is treated to a sundae party after the fair. The cakes are numbered, and the person who wins the cakewalk draws a number from a hat and wins the corresponding cake. Another school designates the best-looking cakes for its bake sale and uses the more ordinary ones for its cakewalk.

Another Virginia school has a cookiewalk, just like a cakewalk, except that there are more winners, and each one wins a cookie instead of a cake. When the music stops, anybody standing on a giant footprint gets a cookie.

Zoo Dip

One of the most profitable and loved activities at a Virginia school, the zoo dip is basically a lottery for stuffed animals. For three tickets, children get one chance at the zoo dip; for five tickets they get two chances. The activity is popular enough to warrant two zoo dips at the fair, each one netting a profit of about $1,000. The following information is based on each zoo dip.

The PTO buys 225 high-quality stuffed animals (ranging from tiny to large), numbers the animals, and lines them up on tables. (Another school used trolls one year, and yet another employed high-quality used stuffed animals donated by school families.) Children reach into a fishbowl containing sealed tickets numbered inside from 001 to 4,000. Anyone who draws a ticket numbered between 001 and 225 wins the corresponding stuffed animal. Fair organizers have worked out the numbers based on past experience, wanting to sell just enough tries at the zoo dip to give away all the animals during fair hours.

The PTO buys the stuffed animals wholesale through a party supplier at a cost of between $2.50 and $50 per animal. Many smaller animals are bought in multipacks, which keeps the average cost to $4.50. Animals are numbered using tie-on tags and displayed on risers so that children can see but not touch them. Four volunteers work at zoo dip on each shift, and since it is a form of gambling, they maintain records (as required by the county) on who wins each animal. Paula Swain says that although zoo dip is a favorite and makes a lot of money, she wouldn't recommend it for a school hosting its first fun fair because of the up-front expense involved.

"JAIL"

At a school in San Antonio, Texas, for two tickets a child can put someone in "jail." The prisoner either has to spend five minutes in jail or must pay a ticket to get out.

AUTO DISPLAY

Try contacting the local branch of a car collector's club to get a vintage auto displayed, or if there's a race track nearby, try to get a race car and trailer to exhibit.

STROLLING CLOWNS/POCKET LADIES/MUFFIN MEN

Children love to see costumed characters walking around at fun fairs, especially those dispensing goodies. When a child gives a ticket to a "pocket lady," the child gets to choose a pocket and keep the treasure found inside, be it a piece of candy, a sticker, or a trinket. At one school, a parent made an inverted tulip costume which is saved and used from year to year. It is a headpiece and matching yellow cape full of pockets inside.

One parent-clown who roves around the fun fair at Noreen Moser's school in Georgia makes balloon animals for children, based on instructions from a book the PTA bought. Another clown gives children "firecrackers"—empty toilet paper rolls filled with candy.

At a Virginia school, parents rent different costumes every year. One year strolling Ninja Turtles were featured and, another time, Disney characters. A volunteer trails each character around the fair and for a dollar's worth of tickets takes a Polaroid picture of a child alongside a character.

BASKETS

A Virginia school has a lot of fun raffling baskets at its fun fair every year. The baskets are filled with items donated by school families, in keeping with suggested themes. The PTA purchases seven large wicker baskets, one for each grade level (K–6), and assigns each grade level a different theme. After five years' experience, the fair's coordinators learned that the basket filled with toys was always the most popular and that the one with food and candy was not well received. They finally settled on the following as the seven best baskets:

sports

arts and crafts

books

school supplies

kitchen and gourmet

travel (small games and so forth)

toys

Parents are asked to send in a new item (in its original packaging) costing about $3, or to chip in together on a larger item or gift certificate. The PTA places decorated paper grocery bags in each classroom for collecting the items and sends home occasional reminders in the school newsletter and fun fair flyer. About two weeks before the fun fair, the items are collected and the arranged baskets placed prominently in a locked display case. This sparks a lot of interest and serves as a reminder to students who have not yet brought in their donations.

Raffle tickets are made up in advance with spaces for the purchaser's name and phone number. Each ticket lists the grade levels, so the purchaser can circle the basket that he or she would like to win.

At the fun fair, the baskets are displayed (out of arms' reach), and one or two volunteers sell raffle tickets for one dollar each. The tickets are deposited in seven shoe boxes (one for each basket) that have been decorated by PTA volunteers.

At the end of the fair, the principal—blindfolded—selects a winning ticket from each box. Alana Long said, "The winner takes home the basket and contents and might never again have to buy school supplies!"

BALLOONS

Some schools sell helium balloons at their fun fairs; some used to kick off their fairs by launching balloons. Once the danger to the environment posed by helium balloons became well-known, however, most schools discontinued selling them, and the national PTA recommended not launching them. In addition to environmental concerns, the balloons posed a problem when young children would accidentally release them or break them, and be terribly disappointed. As a result, tears instead of smiles.

FAMILY GAMES AND CONTESTS

If your fair will be outdoors, you can have lots of family games and competitions. Try a tug-of-war, a parent-and-child sack race, a three-legged race, or relay races.

PERFORMANCES

Performances can be scheduled throughout the day. Send home a notice several weeks or a month in advance asking parents if they have any special talents they'd be willing to share. You might find a ventriloquist, folksinger, puppeteer, or magician among parental talents. You can also approach school groups— the band or orchestra at your school or junior high, local dance, karate, judo, and gymnastic schools—to line up short shows. Marcia DeOteris observes: "Performances by the schoolchildren themselves are the biggest draw. At our school, we found that the crowd swelled and ticket sales were highest around the times of the children's performances."

A group of parents and faculty at one school formed a marionette troupe that performs classic fairy tales at their fun fairs. They charge $1.50 per ticket and captivate their young audiences time and time again.

RIDES AND DUNKING BOOTHS

Pony and donkey rides are favorites at outdoor fairs, as are moon bounces and ball crawls, and the trackless train previously mentioned. You can pay a flat fee for these attractions or let the company that owns them take a share of your ticket sales. Usually the activities come complete with employees to supervise them.

Consider renting a dunking booth. Children love trying to hit their parents and teachers to knock them off their seats into a big bucket of water. Darlene Lexa says that her Texas school made its own dunk-the-teacher booth. Teachers took turns sitting on a box behind an old screen door, and children threw water balloons at the "target." The younger the children, the closer to the target they were allowed to stand.

SALES

Because of the crowds at a fun fair, it's the perfect occasion to sell things, ranging from crafts and plants to T-shirts and mugs. If you have cookbooks left over from last year's fund-raiser, sell them at your fun fair. Refer to Chapter 5 for specifics on organizing each different type of sale. But keep in mind the limitations imposed by a fun fair: space constraints and the overall number of volunteers that you can count on. In the following discussion, I briefly cover sales of crafts, plants, used books and toys, and food and beverages.

A **craft sale** can be successful, but you don't want your fun fair to become a flea market. Rather than devote the entire school gym to a craft fair, set a limit of ten or twelve tables. A New Jersey school rents tables at $35 each to twelve vendors, whom they've carefully screened and selected to try to avoid duplication of merchandise. The vendors set their own prices and keep all the proceeds of their sales. Most important, the PTA tries to select a variety of craftspeople, *including some who offer hands-on activities*. Recently, this school featured someone who charged children a nominal fee to make sand designs in bottles that the kids were allowed to take home. Another vendor sold porcelain figurines, which the children painted and took home. The best crafts displays are those that offer some active, hands-on family fun.

Other schools charge less per table—$15 to $25—and some don't charge a flat fee but rather take a percentage of sales proceeds—10 to 20 percent.

For several months before the fair at one school, parents get together one morning a week to make crafts to sell at the fair. Some schools even sell crafts made by the children in art class, but at one school the practice was discontinued, partly because children were upset if their work did not sell. Now the art teacher puts together a display of children's work, which is positioned prominently at the fair, but not for sale!

A **plant sale** works well in the spring. Expecially around Mother's Day, sales of annuals such as impatiens, geraniums, and begonias are popular at fun fairs. (Refer to Chapter 5 to learn more about planning a plant sale.) Lisa Ryan of Vermont reports that the plant sale is a big draw at her school's spring fair. Parents dig up and donate plants from their perennial gardens—irises, rhubarb, pachysandra, ivy, and saplings, for instance. Everyone so looks forward to being able to buy plants there that the plant sale is the biggest money-maker at this fair.

A Virginia school's fun fair features a greenhouse every year. Local florists are requested to donate something—a flower arrangement, hanging basket or other plant, or gift certificate. The fair usually winds up with about twenty-five donations all told. In addition, parents purchase cut flowers and plants at wholesale prices and resell them at retail prices. When the fair's organizers call to line up parent volunteers, they also ask for donations of food for the bake sale or a plant for the greenhouse. During the fair, they have hourly drawings for prizes in the greenhouse and offer to hold purchases until the end of the fair. Parents sell flowers throughout the school by wheeling wagons full of bouquets. They make about $1,000 from the greenhouse every year.

You won't have the volunteers to stage a full-fledged clothesline sale at your fun fair, but you can offer a nice service and make some money at the same time by holding a sale of **used books and toys** that families have donated. Give the librarian and teachers first pick of the items for sale. At Lisa Ryan's school in Vermont, children get to select a free book after donating a specified number of books. At the end of your fun fair, give away the unsold books free to anyone who wants them. (Read Chapter 4 for more specifics on how to run a sale of this sort.)

At most fun fairs, schools have **food and beverages for sale:** coffee and donuts or bagels in the morning (offering them free to volunteers); hot dogs, pizza, and soda for lunch; and popcorn, cotton candy, and ice cream throughout the day.

Some schools sell nachos (keeping the cheese sauce in a Crock-pot), and some have bake sales.

Kids obviously love this type of carnival food, and it's relatively easy to prepare and serve. (A popcorn or cotton candy machine can be rented from a local rental store.) If you decide to serve pizza, see if you can get a local pizzeria to donate the pies or sell them to you at a discount. Likewise, approach grocery stores to see what they'll donate, and see if you can work through your school cafeteria to purchase in bulk.

Consider also offering healthy alternatives—sandwiches, fruit, chili, and/or soup. At one fair, a vegetarian buffet is served complete with fill-it-yourself pitas. The school makes available recipes for dishes like minestrone soup, macaroni and cheese, and tabouleh salad, and each family signs up to bring in a dish.

If you really want to see children having a good time, set up tables where they can decorate their own cupcakes or make their own sundaes. Ask parents to donate plain, unfrosted cupcakes, and let children frost and decorate them using a variety of toppings: sprinkles, M&Ms, nuts, or candy hearts. Make sure to have plenty of wipes for cleanup and to watch to make sure that nobody goes overboard with toppings! Have plastic bags on hand so children can take their creations home if you don't want them eaten on the spot. A school in Virginia sets up an ice cream parlor where parents dish up "Fun Day Sundaes," topping vanilla ice cream with whatever the customer chooses.

At one recent fair, a school sold blue-on-white mugs designed by one of the parents. The mugs cost the school $1.80 each. They sold for $3, which included an initial cup of coffee and unlimited refills throughout the day. The parent volunteer who designed the mugs—an artist—incorporated a café scene picturing children sitting outdoors under an awning; the awning displayed the name of the café—which was the same as the school's.

At one school, soda was sold in nine-ounce paper cups for fifty cents and in seventeen-ounce commemorative plastic fun fair cups for $1.

Some schools do very well with bake sales at their fun fairs; others ask parents to bake for the cakewalk (described on p. 160) or for the cupcake-decorating table and feel uncomfortable asking for additional baked goods.

SILENT AUCTION

With children around, no one has the patience to sit through a live auction, but silent auctions can work well at fun fairs. Parents can browse through the merchandise, placing bids, then revisit the auction an hour or two later to up their bids. (Refer to Chapter 6 for details on how to run an auction.)

The silent auction at a school fair in Maryland makes over $1,200 each year. Parents contribute their skills, a dinner, or a weekend at their vacation cottage, and local businesses donate goods and services.

Don't be overly ambitious in planning a silent auction; make a realistic estimate of the number of volunteers you'll have, and keep the auction to a manageable size. Remember that space might be a constraint. Mara Green, who was in charge of the silent auction at a recent fun fair, says that her school had too many items—about 180—at its silent auction, which was set up in the hallway. "Parents just didn't have time to look at everything," she reports, "so we're going to make it smaller next time." Keep in mind also that security is a concern; guard against children placing phony bids.

———✶——✶——✶——

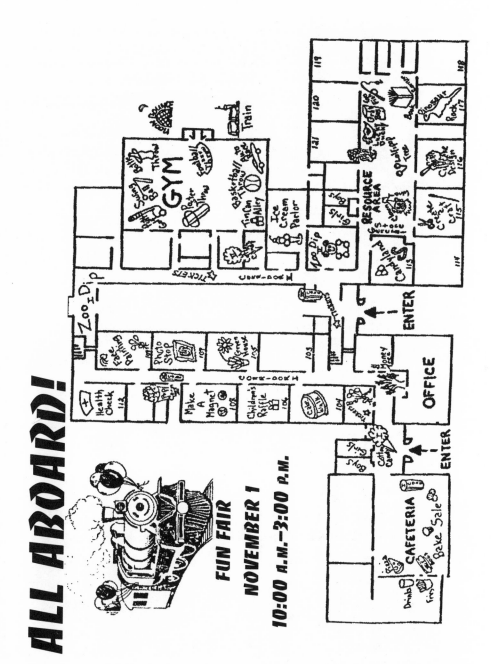

Fall Frolic

OCTOBER 19

SCHEDULE

9:30 A.M.	Registration for Fun Run
10:00 A.M.	One-Mile Fun Run
11:00 A.M.	Booths open Pumpkin pie/specialty contest judging Great Pumpkin appears
11:15 A.M.	Awards for Fun Run
11:30 A.M.	"Animals Nobody Loves": A Presentation by ———————
12:00 NOON	Pumpkin pie/specialty contest awards Great Pumpkin appears
12:15 P.M.	Folksinger ———————
12:45 P.M.	Tae kwon do demonstration
1:15 P.M.	Game/sheet volleyball
1:30 P.M.	"Snakes": A Presentation by ———————
1:45 P.M.	Great Pumpkin appears
2:00 P.M.	Folksinger ———————
2:15 P.M.	Game/ladder relays
2:30 P.M.	Scarecrow contest judging
2:45 P.M.	"Camouflage & Mimicry": A Presentation by ———————
3:00 P.M.	Game/scavenger hunt Pumpkin face judging Great Pumpkin appears
3:15 P.M.	Pumpkin face awards
3:30 P.M	Raffle drawing
3:45 P.M.	Scarecrow contest awards
4:00 P.M.	Closing

IN ADDITION . . .

		CELEBRITY JUDGES
Bake sale	Kid crafts	
Balloons	Prize	———————
Candy sale	Pumpkin face place	———————
Flowers & bulbs	Pumpkins for sale	———————
Grade-level games	Raffle	———————
Food-food-food	Scout games	———————
Mr. Bouncey		———————

CHAPTER EIGHT

FUN FAIRS II: STEP-BY-STEP PLANNING

GETTING ORGANIZED EARLY IS CRUCIAL AND CAN MAKE THE difference between a successful and less-than-fully-successful fair. Because of the magnitude of the task, have two people cochair your fun fair, assisted by the two people who will assume the cochairmanship the next year. Parents who organize a well-run fun fair in Virginia start planning their March fun fair in June of the previous year, hoping to have all the subcommittee heads lined up before school begins in September.

Delegating responsibility is paramount, especially if you're planning to have other major activities, such as a raffle or plant sale, in addition to games and crafts.

As the chair of a New Jersey fun fair puts it: "I think it's crucial to spread out the responsibilities for planning Mayfair—not just because I am a working mom with a workaholic husband, but also because you get better spirit and more cooperation when the workload is spread."

STAGE ONE (NINE MONTHS BEFORE)

Communication with the Principal

At this early stage, the cochairs of the fun fair need to consult with the principal and make the following basic decisions:

date and time of the fun fair

whether to hold it indoors or out

whether to have a theme and what it should be

whether to have activities in addition to children's games and crafts, and if so, what they will be (raffle, silent auction, sales, performances, pony rides, moon bounces, etc.)

In selecting a date for the fun fair, keep in mind that parking might be a problem if the date coincides with that for a sports event or other activity taking place on school grounds.

Be sure that you find out what your obligations will be concerning cleanup and the use of school facilities after hours. Some schools require the PTA to pay utilities and janitorial costs if the building is used when school is not in session, whereas others don't and even supply custodians to work the day of the fair.

Formation of the Committee

After making these decisions, subcommittee chairs must be lined up (one chair is needed for each major activity). At one school, the fun fair committee is quite large, with the following subcommittees:

setup and takedown	ice cream parlor
bake sale	international food
balloons and money	make-a-magnet
tree	zoo dip
beverages	moon bounce/train
book corner	hostesses for after-the-
cafeteria	fair dinner party
cakewalk	photo stop
children's raffle	prizes/games
cotton candy/popcorn	publicity/posters
create-a-craft	room mothers (to line
cupcake design	up volunteers for
face painting	staffing games)
general store	tickets
greenhouse	finance

Another school has a smaller committee, with people in charge of:

publicity	doll hospital
raffle (main and minis)	volunteers
rummage (books and toys)	food
	plant sale
face painting	games
craft tables	cupcake decorating
memorabilia (school insignia sweatshirts, T-shirts, pennants, cups)	vendors
	equipment
	rides

If possible, visit fun fairs at neighboring schools to see how others run such an event. Refer to the chapters on sales of merchandise, auctions, and food and entertainment for detailed pointers about planning and preparing for those activities. (The remainder of this chapter deals with coordinating those activities and planning the games and prizes for the fun fair.)

Insurance and Government Permits

Check with county officials to see whether your PTA needs a permit to sell food, hold a fair, have a raffle, or close off the street. In some areas the PTA has to hire a police officer to direct traffic or generally supervise activities. Check your PTA's insurance policy to see if it's necessary to buy a rider to cover any of the activities, such as pony rides. Consult with the cafeteria staff to find out what rules must be followed when using the kitchen.

Safety Measures

Formulate a plan to have a trained professional on hand to administer first aid if necessary. Marcia DeOteris says: "Although we have been very lucky and no one has ever been hurt at our fair, we've always made provision for it. One year, we asked the Red Cross to send a nurse to provide free blood pressure screenings and also be on hand in case of an emergency. Another year, we had a volunteer ambulance corps present all day. A couple of cups of coffee, lunch, and a heartfelt thank-you were enough payment for these cheerful volunteers."

Volunteers

It's essential to start recruiting volunteers early. You can wait until a month or so before the fair to staff the shifts of volunteers who'll work the actual day of the fair, but long before that you'll need people to assist in the planning and preparation for each major event and activity. Send around sign-up sheets at PTA meetings and make announcements at orientations for new parents, meetings of room parents, and back-to-school night. Have people sign up to work on the subcommittee that interests them: raffle, food, plant sale, performances, volunteer coordination, and so forth. Try to recruit strong people for some of the games, such as moon bounce. And find people who don't mind getting a little messy to sell cotton candy and help with cupcake decorating.

Meeting of the Committee

To keep the committee informed about decisions they've made and the timetable of events, the cochairs should call a meeting to discuss the date, time, physical layout, and theme of the fair. Give subcommittee chairs anything that will help them with their tasks; especially helpful are reports of people who've previously held their jobs. Ideally, there should be a folder for each game or activity prepared by the person in charge of it the year before. This folder would include such explicit "how-to" information that the new subcommittee chair would simply have to decide what he or she wanted to change.

Give the new chairs the names of people who've volunteered to help them and a list of the people chairing the other subcommittees. Distribute a timetable of responsibilities: dates of future meetings and deadlines for submission of notices in fliers. Let them know how to request reimbursement for expenses. (A sample of a list of the general responsibilities that the subcommittee chairs might receive appears at the end of the chapter.)

STAGE TWO (THREE TO FIVE MONTHS BEFORE)

Games and Crafts

At this point, it's not too early to think about the physical layout of the fun fair. When you have a rough idea where each major activity will go, start planning specific games and crafts. If your fair will be indoors, you can follow one school's example of selling food in the cafeteria, having games for the older children in the gym, and having games for younger children in another location (a central "pod"). In the hallways, volunteers sell popcorn and cotton candy, tickets (near each of the two entrances), and tickets for the money tree (right outside the office). All other activities are in individual classrooms. (See the floor plan at the end of Chapter 7.)

After figuring out how much space is available for games and crafts, decide which ones to offer and find people to be in charge of each. Most schools assign responsibility for each game to a different class, so that, for instance, parents in Mrs. Wilson's third-grade class are responsible for making and staffing the clown toss. Most likely, there are more classes than games, so ask some classes to supply volunteers for the food concessions and the fair's other sales and activities.

The people in charge of each game need to write up rules, purchase or gather supplies, and do whatever construction, painting, and decorating is needed. If each subcommittee chair writes up a report of her activities, the job of the chair the following year will be easy by comparison. (For a sample of the form that one school asks its chairs to complete, see the end of the chapter.)

Tickets and Prizes

How much should you charge per ticket? How many tickets will be required to play each game? Will prizes be awarded at each game or at a central prize booth? After making these decisions, select a color for the tickets (a different color from last year's), and estimate the total number of tickets and prizes you should buy.

Each year, one school buys about 5,000 prizes and 3,000

tickets for ten children's games and crafts. Roughly 450 students (60 percent of the school population) attend the fair, and, for the most part, the school charges one ticket per activity and hands out prizes to each player at each game. Another school (of 750 students) uses 100,000 tickets each year. It draws a big crowd and offers about twenty-five games and crafts, charging more than one ticket for most of them. In addition, this school allows people to use tickets to buy food, souvenirs, plants, books, and chances at the raffle.

Plan to have a coffee can or plastic milk jug at each game for ticket collection. If it costs one ticket to play a game, tape one ticket to the jug.

For a ticket each, one school sells white plastic "goody" bags (measuring twelve inches by fifteen inches), which children label with their names and use to carry their prizes. You can probably find a local store willing to donate bags.

Prizes and tickets can be purchased through local party supply stores. (Be careful, though, not to use tickets that are readily available, for you don't want people using tickets not purchased through the school.) Check your yellow pages under "carnival supplies" and "party supplies." Many schools mail-order their prizes from one of the companies listed on p. 184.

Publicity

If this is your school's first fun fair and you're starting out small and inviting only members of your school community, there's no need to begin work on publicity this early. If you want to advertise extensively with posters and newspaper ads or sell souvenir cups, mugs, or T-shirts, now's the time to line up a parent to design a logo. The clown logo that a school used one year for its posters appears at the end of the chapter.

Security

A lot of cash changes hands at fun fairs, so you might want to hire an off-duty police officer to patrol and accompany the person making bank deposits. Ask parents who are police officers to volunteer (out of uniform, of course). At one school, members of the volunteer security patrol wear yellow vests during their one-and-a-half-hour shifts. They make a particular point of keeping an eye on the ticket booths, raffles, and bathrooms (where they check also for plumbing problems). Cash is collected throughout the day and locked in the principal's office.

Cleanup

Cleanup can be a massive undertaking, especially when you need to rely on volunteers. Ask older Boy Scout and Girl Scout troops or a high school service club to help out, or set up a subcommittee of parent volunteers to clean up. Ask the person in charge of each game or craft to bring a broom with her the day of the fair and to sweep and clean up her area at the end of the day, with the help of the last shift of volunteers.

STAGE THREE (TWO MONTHS BEFORE)

Meeting of the Committee

Have a meeting of the entire committee to discuss strategy. Finalize the floor plan for the fair, and announce who will be in charge of each game and craft. Ask each subcommittee chair to submit copy for fliers that will be sent home to school families over the next two months and to say how many volunteers and volunteer hours they'll need. (A sample form for this purpose appears at the end of the chapter.

Decide whether to sell tickets at school the week before the fair. This tactic can alleviate long lines the day of the fair. Some schools presell tickets at a slightly reduced price. Make plans to set up for the fair—the day before if it'll be indoors, or a few hours beforehand if it'll be outdoors. At one school, volunteers set up after school on Friday for a Saturday fair, and they had baby-sitters available to make the job go quickly.

Volunteers

Decide how many shifts of volunteers will be working the day of the fair. Limit each shift to an hour and a half or two hours so parents can enjoy the rest of the day with their children.

Have the last shift end half an hour after the fair closes (to help with cleanup). If each class is to be responsible for a different activity, schedule a meeting of room parents to explain their responsibilities.

Think about ways to make the subcommittee chairs visible the day of the fair—by having them wear school T-shirts or aprons, for example. One school gave them red bandannas and buttons to wear one year and bright-colored fun fair T-shirts another. Plan to set up a spot at the fair where these individuals can retreat for a coffee break.

Plan a postfair social event for the fun fair committee. At one Virginia school, the previous year's cochairs entertain the current year's committee for dinner the evening of the fun fair. The principal, faculty, and other staff who helped out are invited to the party, too. People attending pay a nominal fee to cover the cost of cold cuts or lasagna, and everyone has a chance to unwind together. The cochairs use the occasion to present each committee and staff member with a token gift. Another school has a potluck luncheon a few weeks after the fair. Alana Long, former PTO president, says, "The rule is if you don't hand in your subcommittee report at the luncheon, you chair that subcommittee next year!"

Publicity

Print up copies of posters if you want to advertise outside your school. Hang them in places frequented by people with children: pediatricians' offices, children's shoe stores, toy stores, grocery stores, and so forth.

If you plan to sell cups or mugs with the fun fair logo, have a "stat" copy made at a copy shop, and order the merchandise.

Obtain permission to decorate the school's hallways (and showcase, if you have one) for two weeks prior to the fair. Consider sponsoring a poster contest and using the posters to decorate the halls. At one school, each child who submits a poster gets a few free tickets to the fun fair.

Get clearance to erect a big sign on the school's front lawn, and ask someone to create it. If your school has a public address system, ask if someone can make announcements each day during the week preceding the fair and whether loudspeaker announcements are allowed during the fair. (If the latter are permitted, recruit someone to act as announcer. This is a big job!)

Send home the first fun fair flier, letting parents know about the upcoming fair and asking for help. (An example of such a form appears at the end of the chapter.)

Permits

Apply for any necessary governmental permits.

Communication with School Custodians

The volunteer in charge of arrangements or equipment coordination should be in close contact with the custodians. It might be helpful to use a form like the sample at the end of the chapter; each chair fills it out, letting the custodians and equipment coordinator know exactly what his or her needs will be.

Communication with Teachers

If the fair is going to be indoors, let each teacher know what will take place in his or her classroom and which activity parents in his or her class are responsible for. Remind teachers to prepare their classes the day before the fair. If the fair will be indoors, ask them to have their students move desks to the side, turning them inward to protect the contents.

Tickets and Prizes

Order the tickets and prizes if you haven't already done so.

Rental Contracts

Make arrangements for whatever you plan to rent: a moon bounce, extra tables, popcorn or cotton candy machine, or ponies for pony rides. (Some fast food restaurants donate the use of a moon bounce at no charge, but reservations must be made well in advance.) Be sure to have a rain clause in the contract with the supplier for anything that must be set up outdoors, so that the PTA doesn't have to pay for something that wasn't used.

STAGE FOUR (ONE MONTH BEFORE)

Meeting of the Committee

At this meeting of the entire committee, finalize logistical arrangements for the day of the fun fair. Discuss setup and cleanup. Let people know how they can communicate with the fun fair's chairs during the fair if necessary. (Use walkie-talkies if you can borrow them.) Remind everyone to keep good records for the people in charge next year. (This will make it easier to find people willing to do these jobs next year.) A copy of a memo sent to the subcommittee chairs unable to attend a committee meeting of this sort appears at the end of the chapter.

Request each chair to call her workers a week or so before the fair to remind them of what they volunteered to do and to spell out their duties.

Publicity

Send home another flier about the fair, making sure to coordinate this effort with all subcommittee chairs. You don't want to inundate parents with lots of separate fliers when one will suffice. Submit press releases to local newspapers, and erect a sign on the front lawn of the school. If you have permission to use the school's loudspeaker system, write announcements for the week before and the day of the fair. (Examples modeled after one school's announcements appear at the end of the chapter.)

Finance

Get cashboxes and start-up change for each location at which you'll be taking money: ticket booths, raffle tables, and food concessions. Start saving coffee cans or plastic milk jugs for ticket collection at each game and activity.

Decide where you'll safeguard accumulated cash the day of the fair, and arrange for depositing the money at the bank. Request that everyone submit their expense statements by the day before the fair. That way, you can calculate your profit quickly.

Decide whether you want to analyze each game to determine its profitability. At one school, tickets are collected in milk jugs at each game, and the ticket subcommittee collects and weighs them with a jeweler's scale at the end of the day to calculate how much money each game took in. By subtracting associated expenses, they determine the profit from each game. In deciding what games to offer the next year, they either discontinue unprofitable games or charge more tickets to play them.

At another school, the sixth-graders analyze the profitability of each game. In math class, they estimate and count tickets, create balance sheets, and made recommendations as to the profitability of each activity and sale.

Fun Fair Calendar

At one school, each subcommittee chair gets a calendar of fun fair events and deadlines for the months just before and the month of the fair. A sample of the calendar (for a March 10 fair) appears at the end of the chapter.

STAGE FIVE (SETUP)

The person in charge of each activity is responsible for her own setup. The finance chair has to bring the cashboxes and start-up change. Be sure to have on hand:

coffee and donuts or bagels for the volunteers

permits and insurance papers

buttons/bandannas/T-shirts/aprons for subcommittee chairs

name tags for volunteers

cameras and film

security vests

walkie-talkies and/or bullhorns

lists for volunteers to sign in

If the fair is going to be indoors, make sure that the heat is turned off or set very low. Cordon off areas of the school that are off limits, and lock doors of rooms that won't be used. Place trash cans everywhere. Have cones near the parking lot to reserve at least one parking space should someone on the fair committee need to drive someplace during the event.

STAGE SIX (THE DAY OF THE FUN FAIR)

The day of the fair, the cochairs should have no responsibilities other than to oversee the entire event. They should be stationed at a central spot, with walkie-talkies positioned at strategic locations so that people can let them know about problems, such as having too many or too few volunteers. One cochair can walk around the fair making sure that everything is running smoothly. At a Virginia school, the cochairs try to take a picture of each chair and have the pictures developed in time for the postfair party that evening.

When cleaning up after the fair, save everything that can be reused: signs, rules, leftover tickets, prizes, decorations, supplies, and props for the games themselves. Saving these items will make next year's fair that much easier. Ask if there's a closet at school that can be used for storage. At the end of one fair, the person in charge of each game or craft takes an inventory of what's left over, puts everything in the closet, and tapes the inventory sheet to a box containing leftover supplies.

STAGE SEVEN (A FEW WEEKS AFTER)

Write thank-you notes to all the chairs and school personnel who helped out. Write a general thank-you to the other volunteers, and publish it in the PTA newsletter.

Host a coffee or luncheon for the committee, and ask

people to submit their reports at that time. Deliver these, along with the report of the fair's cochairs, to next year's chairs.

Sharon Gordon, cochair of a large fun fair, offers this advice:

> During the first couple of weeks after the fair, you might experience a personal slump. After running in "5th gear" for so long, all fair-related activity comes to a complete stop. Everyone assumes you need a vacation; no one calls. This is a good time to have plenty of fun, and line up new activities.

Or plan another fair!

——————*—————*—————*————

Companies That Sell Carnival Prizes

Oriental Trading Co., Inc.
P.O. Box 3407
Omaha, Nebraska 68103
1-800-228-2269

Oriental Merchandise
2636 Edenborn Avenue
Metairie, Louisiana 70002
1-800-535-7335

Russ Berrie & Company
(nice stuffed animals)
111 Bauer Drive
Oakland, New Jersey 07436
1-800-272-RUSS

KIPP Brothers, Inc.
240 S. Meridian Street
Indianapolis, Indiana 46206
1-800-428-1153

U.S. Toy Co., Inc.
1227 E. 119th Street
Grandview, Missouri 64030
1-800-255-6124

FUN FAIR

General Responsibilities of the Subcommittee Chairs

1. Carefully *review the material in your subcommittee's Fun Fair folder from last year*, paying special attention to the subcommittee report, to get a feel for the job and the timing involved.

2. *Set up an additional subcommittee* if one is needed; call volunteers from the list provided.

3. *Remember the Fun Fair's train theme*—"All Aboard!"—as you make your preparations, and integrate the two (if only on a small scale) if you can.

4. Try to *attend the two Fun Fair meetings* to stay current on the plans and progress being made.

5. *By the meeting on* _____ , give the Fun Fair cochairs (in writing) your requirements for the space to be assigned to your activity, and inform them whether or not you will need the help of volunteers. If so, we need to know how many, and for which shifts. At this time, also turn in your supplies, materials, and equipment needs to the chair in charge of arrangements.

6. *Personally inspect the space assigned to your activity*, once the draft floor plan of the Fair is drawn up. If it is not satisfactory, let the Fun Fair cochairs know ASAP.

7. *Turn in Fun Fair Flier Information Forms* by the three deadline dates.

8. *Turn in your expenses regularly* so the Fun Fair cochairs will have an ongoing accounting record. All bills are due by _____ .

9. *Set up your activity* on the Friday afternoon or evening before the Fair. On Saturday, bring a broom to assist with cleanup, and make sure your area is left in good condition.

10. *Arrive at the Fair* at least one hour before your activity is scheduled to begin.

11. At the end of the Fair, *inventory your remaining supplies* and materials and securely attach the listing to the outside of the box in which the articles are to be stored.

12. Keep notes throughout your preparations to assist you with your *Fun Fair Subcommittee Report, due* _____ .

FUN FAIR SUBCOMMITTEE REPORT

Please include all details so that future Fun Fairs may benefit from your experience. Use both sides of the paper if necessary.

Subcommittee _____

Chairperson(s) _____ _____

Subcommittee members _____ _____

_____ _____ _____

_____ _____ _____

Fair location _____

Price(s) charged: Number of tickets _____ Cash price $ _____

Income and expenses

Number of tickets collected _____ × $._____   = $ _____

Plus cash receipts   + _____

Less cash float   − _____

Net income   = _____

Less expenses*   − _____

Profit $_____

Supplies and materials (purchased or donated)

Item	Source	Cost
_____	_____	$_____
_____	_____	_____
_____	_____	_____
_____	_____	_____
_____	_____	_____
_____	_____	_____
_____	_____	_____
_____	_____	_____
_____	_____	_____

*Total expenses $_____

(continued)

Subcommittee responsibilities

Three to five months before the Fun Fair:

Two months before:

One to two weeks before:

The previous day:

Fun Fair day: Explain how the activity is set up and run; use diagrams, list materials needed. What do the chair(s), subcommittee members, and volunteers do? How many people are needed; at what time?

Comments

Number of people needed to serve on this subcommittee: _____
What worked well?

What didn't work so well?

Suggestions for next year?

Other comments:

Lincoln School

Saturday, May 1

10:00 A.M. to 3:00 P.M.

Rain or Shine

Free Admission

crafts . . . games . . . entertainment . . . face painting . . . pony
rides . . . plants . . . food . . . raffles . . . vendors

Special performances by

_____Community Band
Lincoln's own Creative I Chorus and Dance
and resident recording artist _____

Mayfair Volunteer Requirements

Indicate your need for volunteers to assist in the operation of your activity.

Use time slots as a guide.

Number
needed

8:00–10:00 A.M. (setup) _____

10:00–12:00 NOON _____

12:00–2:00 P.M. _____

2:00–4:00 P.M. (breakdown 3:00–4:00) _____

Name _____

Activity _____

Do you know anyone who would like to help?

Name _____

Phone _____

If you find that you need to revise your requirements, please contact _____ as soon as you know there is a change.

FUN FAIR MAY 1

Dear Parents:

MEETING
Everyone who signed up to help on a Fun Fair committee (and
everyone who meant to but didn't!) is invited to a short organizational
meeting on _____ in the community room at school. If you are
unable to attend but would like information, please call _____
at _____ .

CAKE DECORATING CONTEST
Enter on _____ and be eligible to win Fun Fair tickets!! Several
winners will be chosen from each grade level. Start thinking of a
unique or beautiful design. . . . Details will be forthcoming.

SILENT AUCTION
Be generous! Be creative! Ask at your place of business for a product
or service to help raise money for our school, or consider donating a
special item yourself, or your time or talents. Ideas include: baby-
sitting, piano/language lessons, tutoring, home-cooked meal, party
planning, boat trip, car wash, calligraphy, use of a weekend home, etc.
The possibilities are endless! Fill out the form below or call _____
at _____ .

WHITE ELEPHANT/USED BOOK SALE
Start looking through your closets for good-quality used books, toys,
and household items and clothing, please. Donations will be accepted
at school all week prior to the fair. Tax receipts will be available. For
more information, call _____ at _____ .

ENTERTAINMENT
We would like to have several "shows" at this year's fair and need
entertainers. If you have a talent or know of an individual or group
who might like to perform (shows will last approximately twenty
minutes), please call _____ at _____ . We are especially interested
in a magician, a puppeteer, a storyteller, a mime, or a karate demo.

BAKE SALE
Local cookie monsters and choc-o-holics are eagerly awaiting the bake
sale! Donations can be dropped off at school on _____ between
_____ and _____ . For more information, call _____ at _____ .

(continued)

VOLUNTEERS
Please check the form below. We still need help on some subcommittees!! Room parents will begin scheduling volunteers to work at games/activities, so please check your preferred time. Notice that this year, we have *one*-hour shifts!!

Name _____

Phone _____

Teacher _____

I would like to donate to the silent auction _____

I will bake _____ cupcakes _____ bread _____ cake

_____ cookies or brownies (wrapped three per bag)

I can help _____ silent auction—contacting business in person/by phone

_____ silent auction—picking up donations

_____ games—selecting

_____ prizes—displaying

_____ white elephant sale—setting up and pricing

_____ used book sale—setting up

_____ room parents—scheduling volunteers for one game or activity

_____ games—setting up Friday afternoon or evening

_____ work 10:00–11:00

_____ work 11:00–12:00

_____ work 12:00–1:00

_____ work 1:00–2:00

_____ work 2:00–3:00

Subject to approval, I would like a personal booth for

_____ .

FUN FAIR EQUIPMENT REQUEST FORM

Name _____

Coordinator of _____

Phone _____

Number of tables needed   _____
Number of chairs   _____
Number of extension cords _____

List any other equipment needed and amount (be specific).

_____

_____

_____

Do you have any special accommodations/location needs?

_____

_____

_____

Is your location on the proposed map satisfactory? If not, please let me know immediately as any change will affect the rest of the floor plan.

_____

_____

_____

Please include any other additional information or needs required to facilitate your setup. _____

_____

_____

Please return this form to the equipment coordinator by _____ .

To: FUN FAIR CHAIRS ABSENT FROM MEETING HELD _____

From: _____

Here is a rundown of the more urgent things that you missed; we would appreciate your response, where needed, ASAP.

- TICKETS will again be six for a dollar prefair, and five for a dollar on Fun Fair day, giving us an average ticket value of about eighteen cents. Please evaluate the costs that you are incurring and determine if you need to raise the number of tickets required to do your activity in order to remain profitable. If so, we need to know right away.

- Your activity, _____ , has been assigned to the following location: _____ . If there is a problem with this SPACE ASSIGNMENT, we must know by _____ .

- Classroom parents from the class of _____ have been asked to STAFF your activity.

- We have white plastic BAGS (twelve inches by fifteen inches) for the children to carry their goodies around in. The price for each will be one ticket. Let us know if you would like to stock them at your booth.

- Do you need a copy of the Fun Fair train LOGO?

- Do you need to have any ANNOUNCEMENTS made over the public address system on the day of the Fun Fair? If so, put them in writing, along with the desired broadcast time, and turn them in by _____ .

- SETUP DAY is _____ . Be sure to line up HELPERS to assist with your activity's setup. We are planning to offer a SITTER SERVICE that afternoon from 3:00 to 6:00 P.M. at the school, at a cost of $2 to $2.50 per child. If you will not be leaving your children at home, let us know how many, and what ages, so we can line up plenty of sitters.

- We need a brief DESCRIPTION OF YOUR ACTIVITY, including the cost to do it (number of tickets and/or cash) for the GUIDE TO THE FUN FAIR. Please write it up and leave it in the Fun Fair folder in the office, along with the Flier #3 message, by _____ . This is the place to "sell" your activity!

- Please call and offer jobs to the VOLUNTEERS listed on the volunteer sheet in your subcommittee chair's folder.

- Do you have any questions about the SUBCOMMITTEE REPORT FORM, also found in your folder? Reports are due on _____ .

- Be sure to turn in your receipts regularly so PTO Treasurer _____ can stay current on our expenditures.

We appreciate the time and effort you are giving to make this year's Fun Fair a success. Thank you!

FUN FAIR ANNOUNCEMENTS

For Week Preceding the Fair

Friday
TICKETS FOR THE FUN FAIR WILL BE ON SALE STARTING MONDAY. Buy your tickets early: six tickets for a dollar every morning before school next week. Price goes up on the day of the Fair.

Remember: to win one of the fantastic prizes in the children's raffle, you can start stuffing the boxes Monday.

I REPEAT: TICKET SALES AND CHANCES AT WINNING THE CHILDREN'S RAFFLE START MONDAY.

Monday
Tickets for the Fair will be on sale again tomorrow morning—six tickets for only one dollar!! The new event Photo Stop requires ten tickets to have your picture taken with Roger Rabbit, Batman, and/or your buddies. This photo would be a priceless memory of your journey through the Fun Fair!!

Tuesday
Remember to get your tickets for the Fun Fair at six tickets for one dollar.

Take a chance on winning Game Boy, Barbie, Super Mario 3, or a $50 shopping spree at _____ ! Put tickets in the children's raffle boxes.

This year you can stop in at the Fun Fair's Ice Cream Sundae Parlor and have a delicious sundae for five tickets.

Wednesday
Sixth-graders remember: only three days left to bake, bake, bake those cakes for cakewalk. Remember, the class with the most cakes wins ice cream sundaes.

Only two more days to buy tickets for the Fair at the reduced rate of six tickets for a dollar.

Thursday
Tomorrow is your last day to buy tickets for the Fun Fair at the great price of six for one dollar.

Remember: if you'd like to have a favorite photo made into a magnet, bring the picture with you to the Fair.

Fun Fair Announcements For Day of the Fair

10:00 A.M.
WELCOME TO FUN FAIR!

Take your chance at Lucky Ducky, Clown Toss, Lollipop Tree, and other games of luck in the pod.

Take the challenge at Auto Race, Putt Golf, Bottle Throw, and games of skill in the gym.

Jump in the moon bounce, or ride the express train just outside the gym.

Make a magnet, design your own cupcake, create-a-craft.

Win a stuffed animal at our two Zoo Dips.

All these activities and more are at the Fair—have fun!

10:15

Attention all Roger Rabbit fans! Drop by Photo Stop, room _____ , and get a chance to win an eight-foot poster of Roger himself! Two posters, that's two winners each hour. Just come get your picture taken, and sign up to be a winner at the raffle.

Don't forget to stop by the Greenhouse to buy a raffle ticket. Tickets are fifty cents. Greenhouse will be raffling off one prize *each* hour. *You* could win a $20 gift certificate from a local nursery or a topiary fuschia.

10:55

The cafeteria opens in just five minutes. Beat the crowds and enjoy pizza, hot dogs, french fries, lemonade, iced tea, orange drink, or coffee.

All delicious bake sale items are in the cafeteria. For this special day, you can start lunch with dessert!!!!!!!

FUN FAIR
CALENDAR OF EVENTS

January	10	Fun Fair meeting—9:30 A.M.
	24	Flier #1 deadline
	31	Flier #1 published
February	7	Flier #2 deadline
	9	Meeting—9:30 A.M.
	14	Flier #2 published
	20–23	Posters turned in
	21	Flier #3 deadline
	28	Lawn sign erected
	28	Flier #3 published
March	1	Posters hung
	5–9	Ticket sales
		Children's raffle ticket sales
	9	Setup
	10	"All Aboard!": Fun Fair 10:00 A.M.–3:00 P.M.
		Postfair Celebration—7:00 P.M.
	23	All bills due in
	30	Coffee—9:30 A.M. Subcommittee reports due

CHAPTER NINE

FOOD AND ENTERTAINMENT

Bette Lo-Presti, a Florida teacher (and also a parent), says of her school's annual spaghetti dinner: "It may seem like a lot of work for a profit of only $800, but as a teacher I feel that parental involvement in the school is very important. There is a great feeling of camaraderie at the dinner. Parents, teachers, and the principal work together to cook and serve. This good rapport carries over into other important projects."

The social events described in this chapter often don't bring in the biggest sums of money, but, along with fun fairs, they are the fund-raisers that everyone loves best. Here are some proven ideas for parties and performances, and detailed information about hosting a spaghetti or pizza dinner, ice cream social, or pancake breakfast.

PERFORMANCES

Schools sponsor all sorts of performances: productions by students, parents, teachers, musicians, magicians, authors, puppeteers, and acting troupes. When held during the school day, of course, no admission is charged, but when held during the evening or on a weekend, these performances can be fund-raisers.

Student Talent Shows

A Miami elementary school raised about $500 at its talent show by charging $2 admission and selling refreshments. Children auditioned, and a teacher selected those who would be in the show, trying to get a variety of acts: dancing, singing, instrument playing, juggling, and acting.

Jan Smith organized a talent show at her children's elementary school in New Orleans: "By combining the acts, I used every kid who auditioned. I had ten to twelve girls wanting to dance to rock music, so I got them together and asked them to select a piece of music and make up a dance to go to it. They had a ball. I combined four clarinet players into one act, and they played three songs. I had another dozen kids who wanted to do something but who lacked musical training. They got together and wrote a skit spoofing the teachers." Teachers and parents who wanted to perform were welcome. The grand finale was a womanless wedding staged by PTA dads, the principal, and several teachers. Jan rehearsed with the children, and the adults rehearsed on their own. All told, the show ran an hour and a half to a sell-out crowd. The PTA raised close to $2,000 charging admission and selling popcorn and soda.

Parent Productions

At an elementary school in Illinois, parents annually raise $4,000 for the school by staging an original musical. The show, held in the school auditorium, runs on Thursday, Friday, and Saturday nights for two weekends, and all performances are sold out. Admission is $6 per adult, $3.50 for each child.

In May, a committee begins to write the script for the next year's show, which it finishes by September for a late February show date. Auditions are held at the beginning of January, and everyone who tries out gets a part. Rehearsals are two evenings a week and all day Sunday for two months.

This school has an enrollment of 400, and over 150 parents become involved in the production in one capacity or another. The principal and some of the teachers also help. PTO President Linna Cohen says, "It's amazing how many untapped talents parents often have." Two parents cochair the production, and people are in charge of the script, production (set construction and costume design), the stage (lighting and sound), and business (money, tickets, ushers, and refreshments). The PTO hires a professional director, costing about $500, and a four- or five-person band, costing about $1,100.

Teacher Follies and Other Fun Events

What student doesn't love to see his or her teacher perform? The faculty at many schools delight audiences with teacher follies, talent shows, and fashion shows. At a school in upstate New York, the teachers put on an "Amelia Bedelia" fashion show, based on the popular protagonist in a well-known series of children's books. Each teacher dressed outlandishly in "Amelia Bedelia" fashion. For instance, the art teacher fashioned herself a gigantic sun, which she wore as a "sun dress," complete with a pair of three-foot sunglasses.

Teachers in a Michigan community put on a slide show at their middle school's end-of-the-year ice cream sundae night. Slides of the children taken throughout the school year were shown in a show set to music.

A 600-student school in New Jersey sponsors a play or puppet show every year on a Sunday afternoon to kick off its book fair. After paying expenses (for the performers and custodians), the school nets about $1,000 from the show, held in the school auditorium. The PTA charges $4 per ticket, and typically about 400 people attend. Afterward, guests are served apple juice and baked goods donated by parents, and the book fair begins.

Preparations for the performance are minimal. The PTA signs a contract with the performers about four months in advance and begins advertising the show in its newsletter about that time. Two months before, the PTA makes custodial arrangements; one month before, it sends home a flier about the show; and two weeks before, it sends home a flier with a tear-off reservation form. Parents distribute tickets as prepaid reservations come in and also sell tickets at the door. Someone sends the performers directions and asks them their specific needs in terms of stage setup and refreshments. The day of the show, four volunteers collect tickets at the door, and five help at the reception and with cleanup. Most performers charge a flat fee plus travel expenses and require a deposit in advance and the remainder of the payment the day of the show.

You must usually begin selecting a performing group at least six months ahead of time. Preview acts by attending a PTA showcase of the arts, at which many performers each give ten- or fifteen-minute excerpts from their shows. Perhaps there's a local organization where you live that arranges previews, collects ratings and reviews, and compiles the information for its members, for a nominal fee of about $25 per year. Seek recommendations from people in charge of programming for the arts at neighboring schools and theaters. Ask at local bookstores and the library about authors who live nearby, and contact publishers about bringing other authors to school.

An elementary school in Newburgh, New York, holds family movie nights. The PTA rents a children's movie, charges a nominal fee for admission, and sells popcorn. Since it costs about $100 to rent a movie, see if you can share the movie—and the cost—with another school. A "home video" night is another possibility.

PARTIES

Family Roller-skating

A school in Fremont, California, held a roller-skating party that wasn't much work and was definitely a fun family night even if not a big money-maker. The parent organizers arranged to have exclusive use of a roller rink for an evening. Families bought tickets in advance through the school at a discount ($3 per skater for admission, including skate rental). This school made about $1 per skater, for a total profit of $450.

Joan Nurge, who helped organize the occasion, says, "It was fun—a great social and family event." But she cautions: "Check your PTA insurance to see if this type of event is covered, and make sure to obtain a signed disclaimer from participants. Our PTA needed to obtain extra insurance for it."

Family Square Dancing

When Fredda Regen's children attended elementary school, the Connecticut school hosted a harvest party for families. Parents and kids square-danced, and the PTA served cider and donuts and sold pumpkins. By charging a nominal admission fee, the PTA was able to defray expenses and raise a small sum for the school.

All-Adult Evening

You can charge admission to an all-adult dance, dinner, or mystery night. Make the evening fun by giving it a "fifties" or "sixties" theme, or add to the allure by holding it someplace other than school. (Bear in mind that at some schools, alcohol cannot be served on the premises.) A Virginia school held a party in the model home of a new development of spacious houses. Another holds an annual Valentine's Day dinner dance at a country club.

An elementary school in New Jersey held a mystery night. A parent wrote the script, featuring the murder of the school principal, who walked around dressed as a ghost all evening long. Among the suspects was a disgruntled mother whose child hadn't been assigned the teacher she wanted! Parents were given clues throughout the evening, and at the end they voted to decide "whodunnit." Parents paid an admission fee to attend, but the school made most of its money selling advertising space in a journal published for the evening. (See Chapter 10 for a description of that method of soliciting funds directly.)

SPAGHETTI DINNERS, ICE CREAM SOCIALS, AND PANCAKE BREAKFASTS

If your school has a cafeteria, you're all set to host a spaghetti dinner, pizza party, ice cream social, or pancake breakfast. Follow the lead of a California school, where the PTA serves pizza before the school's open house. Draw parents to your book fair as they do in Reston, Virginia, by hosting a spaghetti dinner one evening during the fair. Get dads involved in the PTA by putting them in charge of a pancake breakfast.

What Should You Serve?

Select a menu that's inexpensive, easy to prepare, and enjoyed by children and adults alike. Offer a vegetarian option.

DINNER

At dinnertime, most schools choose to serve pizza or spaghetti, but you could select a different menu, such as chili, chicken, tacos, or lasagna. Although it involves a little extra work, serve salad as well. Working through its school cafeteria, a school in Virginia paid only $25 for salad to feed 500 people—and it came washed and cut up! For dessert, ask parents to donate baked goods, or serve ice cream.

The annual spaghetti dinner at an elementary school in Florida features a simple menu: spaghetti with tomato or meat sauce, salad, garlic bread, and dessert. The tab is $6 for adults and $4.50 for children. (See pp. 208–13 for step-by-step planning and preparation on how to go about having a spaghetti dinner.)

The PTA at a 450-student school in northern California recently began a new tradition: serving pizza and soda to families the evening of the school's open house. This "FUN-raiser," as they call it, brought in only a couple of hundred dollars profit but made it much easier for families to attend open house.

"It was a great idea," reports the organizer. "People coming to the open house didn't have to worry about getting home and cooking dinner and getting out to the school. I think it helped us get the 85 percent parent turnout at open house."

Only a few parents were needed for the pizza sale, which lasted one hour, from 5:30 to 6:30 P.M. The PTA didn't even advertise the sale in a separate flier; it was simply mentioned in the information sent home about the open house. That evening, four parents did it all: One warmed the pizza, one served it, one handed out cans of soda, and one took money. The school goes from kindergarten through second grade, after which students go to another school. Parents from each school volunteered at the other's pizza sale.

The PTA worked through a local pizzeria, which supplied fresh, ready-to-bake pizzas at $6 each, as well as a pizza oven and warmer at no added charge. The pizzeria estimated how many pizzas would be needed for the event the first year. The second year, the PTA ordered thirty-five eight-slice pizzas and sold them by the slice. As it turned out, they had ordered five more pizzas than they needed, and they sold those as whole pies at the end. (The slices were large, and many people split slices for their kids.)

The pizzeria delivered supplies before the sale and picked up the warmer and oven afterward, and the cafeteria staff didn't have to do anything. PTA volunteers cooked the pizzas in the cafeteria on the afternoon of the sale and then warmed them up in the evening. They charged fifty cents for a can of soda or juice and $1.50 for a slice of pizza. Each family took its food outdoors to eat at a picnic table and cleaned up afterward.

DESSERT

If you're serving only dessert, it's simplest to serve ice cream or frozen yogurt. An elementary school in Michigan hosts an annual ice cream sundae night. Fathers scoop the ice cream, and mothers add the guest's choice of toppings. The PTA buys its ice cream at a discount through a local grocery store and asks parents to donate toppings.

You can buy ice cream and even rent a freezer through a local dairy (check your yellow pages under "ice cream and frozen desserts"). The cost of a freezer is usually nominal, and with one you don't have to worry about finding enough freezer space elsewhere. Working through a local dairy, a school in upstate New York purchased seven tubs of ice cream and served 300 people at its ice cream social. (The dairy said that each tub would serve sixty to seventy people, but the volunteers who scooped must have been generous!)

At one school's ice cream socials, guests are served efficiently: They move through one of two identical buffet lines in the cafeteria, first picking up napkins, plastic banana boats, and spoons. They select their ice cream flavors and toppings. Volunteers in each line scoop the ice cream, one scooping each flavor, and others are stationed one to a topping: strawberries (previously frozen), crushed pineapple (canned), chocolate sauce (in plastic squeeze bottles), butterscotch sauce, whipped cream (in squirt cans), and sprinkles.

Hosting an international dessert café is a more complicated endeavor. An elementary school in Poughkeepsie, New York, hosted a café of this type in conjunction with its international fair. It was held on a warm spring evening, and guests paid a flat fee entitling them to a drink and choice of desserts, all baked by parents. Recent immigrants baked desserts from their homelands, and others used old family recipes. The net effect was a delicious and varied array of desserts representing recipes from all over the world. People ate at tables outdoors.

In a section of the parking lot, the physical education teacher provided entertainment: Children performed international folk dances. School projects created for the international fair were displayed throughout the school. The café raised a few hundred dollars, but the money was incidental to the feeling of camaraderie that the event generated.

If your school decides to have a "dessert café," ask parents to label their desserts and send in the recipes as well. Compile the recipes in a cookbook, or have copies of them on hand to give out upon request.

Consider combining a café with entertainment. If your school band needs to raise money to fund a trip, for example, turn your cafeteria into a café and charge admission for an evening of dessert and music performed by—the band!

PANCAKE BREAKFAST

Pancakes are a real crowd-pleaser. A New Jersey school raises more than $1,000 at the pancake breakfast it hosts on a Saturday morning every October. Fathers cook pancakes and sausage outdoors on a large rented grill. Two fathers and two mothers make up the planning committee, and one of them wears a tuxedo and serves as maître d' at the breakfast. Guests are seated indoors, where teachers take their orders for juice, tea, or coffee and serve them platters of pancakes and sausage. The fee is $3 for breakfast, free for children under six. Reservations must be made in advance, so the committee knows how much food to buy. They buy their ingredients and supplies at a local grocery store at a discount and use disposable plates, cups, and silverware to make cleanup easier. Breakfast is served from 8:30 A.M. to 11:30 A.M., facilitating staggered arrivals and adequate seating.

How Many People Can You Feed, and Where Should You Seat Them?

Your principal knows how many people can be seated in your cafeteria or multipurpose room. Be innovative and think of ways of seating even more people—perhaps outside, weather permitting.

If space is still a constraint, you have two options: Maintain long enough hours to accommodate multiple seatings, or admit people by prepayment only and make sure that the number of tickets sold does not exceed the number of seats available. If you admit only people who've prepaid, though, you run the risk of angering those who inevitably show up at the door without reservations. (Three hundred people showed up at a school ice cream social, although only 150 had made reservations.) As a compromise, prepare extra food and admit people at the door, space permitting.

At its spaghetti dinner, a Virginia school serves 500 people over a two-hour period, with 150 to 200 people eating at any one time. People with small children tend not to tarry at mealtimes, especially if they plan to attend a book fair or open house immediately afterward.

How Many Volunteers Do You Need?

You probably won't need as many volunteers as you'd imagine to have a simple dinner, breakfast, or dessert. You'll need a small group to plan and shop, a few people to sell and take tickets at the door, and crews for cooking, setup, serving, and cleanup.

The evening of one Florida school's spaghetti dinner, for instance, about twelve to fifteen volunteers work cooking, serving, and cleaning up.

How Can You Involve Students and Teachers?

Go ahead, just ask them! Ask students and teachers for help. Ask the art teacher if students could make placemats and/or centerpieces. Ask members of high school service clubs to help out. Ask teachers to wait on tables, take tickets at the door, or scoop ice cream. Ask for volunteers to handle specific tasks, and then reward them with a free meal or dessert.

How Much Should You Charge?

Estimate how much it will cost to feed each person, and then decide how much to mark up the cost of admission. Keep the price below or in line with what people would have to pay to get the same meal at an informal restaurant. Don't set the price so high as to exclude families of modest means. Most schools don't expect to raise more than a few hundred dollars at a pizza or spaghetti dinner, their motivation usually being as much social as financial.

How Should You Sell Tickets?

To get an idea of how many people will be attending (so you know how much food to buy), you'll need to sell tickets in advance. A week or two before the event, send home a flier asking parents to submit their reservations and payment in a specially marked envelope.

At one school, the PTA buys large rolls of two-part tickets from an office supply store for about $6.00 per roll (one color for adults, one for children). Tickets are numbered, making it easy to keep an exact head count. A PTA volunteer sells tickets in the cafeteria before school for a few days before the spaghetti dinner.

Children become eligible to win door prizes by depositing one part of their tickets into a bag or box. (They write their names on the back of the ticket.) A PTA volunteer puts the other part of each ticket into an envelope, writing the child's name on the front and handing it back to him or her to take home. (The tickets can be stapled to the same envelope that the child used to bring in the reservation form and check.)

Should You Give Prizes?

Many schools give door prizes, centerpieces, or items donated by parents or area merchants. One school has given extra desserts to people who dress in accordance with the evening's theme. Wearing school colors earned diners an extra cookie when the theme was school spirit; when the theme was crazy hats, wearing a hat did the same.

Where Should You Buy Food and Supplies?

First, try to get whatever you can for free. Kelly Robinson, in charge of a chicken barbecue for a preschool in Vermont, says: "I had never asked for donations before, and I was overwhelmed by the response. Farmers and storekeepers asked what did I need and how much!" Fast-food restaurants often donate juice for school functions.

Ask parents what they can donate. Parents at a school in Florida donate raw spaghetti, desserts, and door prizes for their spaghetti dinner. And a parent who owns a pizzeria in Michigan donates all the pizzas for his school's annual pizza dinner.

Failing a donation, ask stores to sell you ingredients at a discount because you're a school group. One parent said that the local supermarket gave her school a 5 percent discount, which didn't seem like much but added up fast at the checkout. Since you're buying in bulk, you can also benefit by shopping at a warehouse store.

Don't forget your own school cafeteria. Patty Gehring, in charge of a spaghetti dinner in Virginia, recommends that you "always to work through your cafeteria." The cafeteria staff buys food in bulk and prepares it in quantity every day. They can either put you in touch with their suppliers or place orders themselves.

What Health Code Regulations Pertain?

Check to see what state, county, and school district regulations must be followed. In some cases, a cafeteria employee must be present at all times when the school kitchen is in use or to turn on appliances. Food that parents send in from home must be closely monitored. It might be better to confine parent contributions to baked goods rather than salads and main courses. You don't want food poisoning to "spoil" your affair; regardless of regulations, make sure to refrigerate perishable food.

What Should Be Done with Leftovers?

Donate leftovers to a soup kitchen or shelter for the homeless. If only baked goods remain, consider wrapping them up for the school's faculty and staff.

STEP-BY-STEP PLANNING AND PREPARATION FOR A SPAGHETTI DINNER

Stage One (Six Months Before)

Form a small committee, with people in charge of:

> publicity
> food and supplies
> tickets, reservations, and finance
> volunteers
> decorations and setup
> cleanup

The committee should meet to select a menu and date for the dinner. Clear everything with the principal, and discuss arrangements for using the school after hours. Find out if the PTA has to pay for using the kitchen, utilities, and custodial help and what health regulations must be heeded.

Stage Two (Two Months Before)

Meet with the committee and decide:

> whether to have a theme and what it should be
> whether to give door prizes

whether to have entertainment

how to involve students and faculty

Brainstorm to draw up a list of people to ask to donate food.

PUBLICITY

Put an article in your PTA newsletter telling everybody when the spaghetti dinner will be.

FOOD AND SUPPLIES

Speak to the person in charge of your school cafeteria to learn the rules concerning use of this facility. Ask for help figuring out how much food to buy and whether you can purchase it through the cafeteria.

Most schools serve guests buffet-style by having them go through the cafeteria line as the children do at lunchtime. If this is the approach you choose, decide what kind of trays to use— cafeteria or disposable.

Decide what to serve for dessert and whether to ask people to bake desserts.

TICKETS, RESERVATIONS, AND BANKING

Purchase the tickets for the dinner. (See earlier discussion on p. 206 about what type of tickets to buy.) Decide whether to limit the number of people you will serve and how to get an idea of how many to expect.

Stage Three (One Month Before)

PUBLICITY

Send home a flier telling about the spaghetti dinner and asking for volunteer help. (See the sample flier at the end of the chapter.)

FOOD AND SUPPLIES

Decide how to cook the spaghetti and sauce and what pots to use. You can cook all the spaghetti before the dinner and plunge it into boiling water for a minute or two to warm it up just before serving it.

Make shopping lists for food and supplies. Check the PTA's supply closet to see what you already have. One school buys paper dinner plates, plastic silverware, five-ounce disposable bowls for salad, paper trays, and two paper napkins per guest.

Patty Gehring recommends buying "enough spaghetti and sauce to feed 600, and that'll be just the right amount to feed 500." Her school gets "one container of meatless sauce and the rest with meat. Most people prefer sauce with meat."

Decide what beverages to serve. If you're going to buy drink concentrate from a fast-food restaurant, place your order and reserve the jugs that you'll need. Gehring's school reserves three jugs and buys five bottles of orange drink concentrate for 500 people. Most restaurants supply 100 paper cups with each container of drink mix. Gehring purchases a jar of unsweetened, decaffeinated iced tea powder at a grocery store and mixes it up to have another drink to offer.

Place orders for bread, salad, and ice cream. To feed 500, Gehring orders eighty-five loaves of French bread and gets twelve slices per loaf. Make arrangements to purchase salad. Forty pounds of salad and one gallon of salad dressing will feed 500. Ask the cafeteria staff or parents for big pans to use for serving salad at the dinner. Gehring's school serves ice cream cups and cookies for dessert, figuring on one cup and two cookies per person. She has found that 60 percent of people prefer vanilla ice cream, 40 percent chocolate.

TICKETS, RESERVATIONS, AND FINANCE

Decide the procedure you'll use to presell tickets and whether you'll also sell tickets at the door. (See p. 206 for a description of how one school presells tickets.)

Volunteers

Schedule volunteers to:

> sell tickets
>
> cook
>
> set up
>
> serve
>
> clean up
>
> buy ingredients and supplies in advance
>
> pick up the bread the day of the dinner
>
> pick up the jugs, ice, and drinks from the fast-food restaurant and return the empties

At Gehring's school, the two hours of the spaghetti dinner are divided into one-hour shifts, with about twelve volunteers working each. A few other people help with cleanup and setup, and one person sells advance tickets before school.

Stage Four (One to Two Weeks Before)

Publicity

Send home a flier inviting people to the spaghetti dinner and instructing them how to purchase their tickets in advance. (A sample flier appears at the end of the chapter.)

Food and Supplies

Purchase whatever food and supplies you can in advance.

Tickets, Reservations, and Finance

Presell tickets, and deposit the money in the bank. Reimburse parents for expenses they've already incurred.

VOLUNTEERS

Do the final scheduling of volunteers. Let volunteers know what their exact responsibilities will be, and suggest that each wear an apron. (A sample of a letter that might be sent to student volunteers appears at the end of the chapter.)

DECORATIONS AND SETUP

Finalize plans for decorations and setup. Check with the cafeteria staff to find out when you can set up.

CLEANUP

Call to find out if the local soup kitchen would like any leftover food. Make sure to have a subcommittee to help with cleanup, deliver the leftover food, and return the empty drink jugs.

Stage Five (The Day of the Spaghetti Dinner)

DECORATIONS AND SETUP

Decorate the cafeteria, and set up the buffet line, with silverware and napkins, trays, and plates at the beginning. Arrange it so that people will first be served spaghetti, then sauce, salad, bread, dessert, and Parmesan cheese. Place drinks at a separate table in the cafeteria. Set up a table at the door for ticket sales. Put placemats at each place, and you're all set.

FOOD AND SUPPLIES

Pick up food that you must get at the last minute. If you're using drinks from a fast-food restaurant, pick up the drink concentrate and jugs, filled with ice if possible. Make sure to bring along a deposit check, which will be returned to you when you give back the jugs.

Arrange desserts on platters. Precook the spaghetti, and arrive at school an hour before the dinner to start heating up sauce, boiling water, dressing and dishing out the salad.

At the dinner, have two volunteers filling plates with noodles and handing them to two others who spoon on sauce and give the plates to the guests. Three volunteers should work on salad: Two fill the bowls, and one gives each guest a filled bowl. Have one person hand out ice cream and two hand out baked goods. (Without volunteers stationed at the desserts, you might run out early!) Two volunteers can act as runners to fill serving containers with food from the refrigerator, stove, and warmers. Have two people pour juice and a few people on hand to make sure that messes are cleaned up as people finish and leave. These people should be equipped with dishpans and sponges.

TICKETS, RESERVATIONS, AND FINANCE

Have a few people on hand to sell and take tickets at the door and direct traffic. Make a bank deposit.

CLEANUP

Clean up the kitchen and cafeteria, and deliver leftovers. Immediately return the empty jugs to the fast-food restaurant. Otherwise, they'll get very sticky.

Stage Six (One to Two Weeks After)

Make sure to thank everyone who contributed to make the dinner a success: parent, teacher, and student volunteers, merchants who donated food and supplies, the principal, and custodial and cafeteria staffs. Let everyone know how much money the school made.

Write up a report to be used by the person who chairs the dinner the next time.

———— ✳ —— ✳ —— ✳ ————

FOURTH ANNUAL FAMILY SPAGHETTI DINNER

Tuesday, November 1

5:30–7:30 P.M.

The Spaghetti Dinner has been a huge success each year. We all have a great time. It is time to start putting everything together for this year's event!!!! We always need volunteers. We always get such wonderful help for this event. If there is anything you can volunteer to do, please fill out and return this sheet.

The following supplies and help are needed:

********BAKED GOODS FOR DESSERT
********DONATIONS FOR DOOR PRIZES (START TALKING TO LOCAL
        MERCHANTS, AND ALSO SEE IF YOU HAVE ANYTHING AT HOME
        YOU WOULD LIKE TO DONATE)
********THIN SPAGHETTI
********YOUR TIME: PREPARING FOOD, SETTING UP, SERVING,
        OR CLEANING UP

Please return this form to school. Remember: All proceeds go to our kids.
Thank you for your help. If you have any questions, please call_____.

Name _____

Phone number_____

I would like to:

_____

_____

_____

_____

YOU'RE INVITED TO AN EVENING OF
GREAT FOOD AND FUN

The Annual
Lincoln PTA
Spaghetti Dinner

When: Tuesday, November 1, 5:00–8:00 P.M.

Where: The School Cafeteria

Cost: Adults $4.00
          Children 3—12 . . . . $3.00
          Children under 3 . . . . . . Free

ADVANCE TICKET PURCHASE IS RECOMMENDED.

Tickets will be sent home with your child on the day of purchase. Ticket sales will be from 8:45 to 9:30 A.M. in the school cafeteria on the four school days preceding the date of the Spaghetti Dinner. Ticket sales will be limited to the first 500 people. There is no guarantee that tickets will be available at the door on Tuesday, November 1. Please purchase your tickets early.

******Homemade Cookies by ——— Student Groups******

Show Your School Spirit—Wear a Hat and Receive an Extra Cookie

Tear off and send with your check (to Lincoln School PTA) or cash.
Yes!! We're coming to the Spaghetti Dinner.

Child's name _____   Teacher _____

——— Adults @ $4.00 ea. $———

——— Children 3–12 @ $3.00 ea. $———

                              TOTAL $———

Duties of a Safety Patrol at the Spaghetti Dinner

1. Please be in the cafeteria at the appointed time.

2. Report to the position you have been assigned to.

3. Jobs:
   - Clear tables, replace mat if needed, put new set of silverware at each place, clean up any messes (if major, please have an adult help you).
   - Pour juices and refills at the juice table.
   - Take tickets at the cafeteria door.
   - Carry out trays for families that need help.

4. You are entitled to a dinner after you work for the first shift and before you work if you have the second shift. Please take only one ice cream and three cookies so we have enough for all our diners. Thank you very much and have a good time.

Name _____

Shift _____

Position _____

CHAPTER TEN

CONTRIBUTIONS FROM THE SCHOOL COMMUNITY (PARENTS, ALUMNI, BUSINESSES, AND NEIGHBORS)

"**L**AST YEAR, OUR SCHOOL SOLD CANDY AND SNACK FOODS. When the products arrived, they were a lot smaller and not as nice as indicated in the brochures. I am getting to the point where I don't want to buy another item. If the school needs $20, ask me. It's certainly better than spending $40 or more on something I don't want," says Susie Herrera of Camarillo, California.

In an effort to raise large sums of money, and in response to the concerns of parents who share Susie's feelings and a shortage of volunteers to staff fund-raising events, many public schools have begun to ask parents to make contributions directly to the school. This request is sometimes made with the understanding that if enough funds are raised, no other fund-raisers will be needed.

Direct solicitation can be surprisingly effective in getting support from parents, alumni, local businesses, and people who live in the district but who don't have children in school. Here are some ideas that work:

MONEY TREE/WALL OF RECOGNITION

"Our PTA promised not to sell anything all year if there was enough support for the money tree at school. Different amounts of money represented different-colored leaves on the tree. The lowest donation was $1, and the highest was $50. Some parents got a single leaf for the family and others a leaf for each child. The tree was very colorful in its fall foliage, and it was GREAT not to have to sell anything," says Jane Larke of Houston.

A 475-student school in Thousand Oaks, California, conducted its first drive for direct contributions a couple of years ago, raising $3,300. The PTA conducted a survey of parents and found overwhelming support for this approach. "The survey indicated that parents would prefer to make a onetime flat donation rather than being bothered with lots of little fundraisers throughout the year," reports Helene McCabe. "We will still have three other large fund-raisers—a gift wrap sale, a knowledge-a-thon, and a PTA membership drive." (A letter that a PTA might send home to parents appears at the end of the chapter.)

PENNY DRIVES

On a smaller scale, you can have a penny drive, asking children to bring in pennies to fill up a jar in each classroom or to try to cover the gym floor. If each of 500 children brings in $3 in pennies, your school will raise $1,500. Use a penny drive as an educational exercise: Ask students to estimate how many pennies have been collected, count the pennies by twos, fives, and tens, graph each classroom's contribution, and then bundle the coins into coin wrappers.

NONPROFIT FOUNDATION

In La Cañada, California, parents set up a nonprofit foundation to raise funds for the entire school district. The Save Our Schools Foundation (SOS), which is independent of the PTA, raised $450,000 in the 1991–92 school year in a central school district of 3,400 students.

In California, 90 percent of school funding comes from the state, and SOS attempts to bring in enough funds to keep class size below the state average and offer enhanced programming. A variety of approaches is used to this end, most notably through requests to businesses, parents, and other residents for direct contributions. "Our parents expect a lot from the schools, yet in turn they give a lot in terms of their time, effort, and money," says the foundation vice president, Lettice Carroll.

The campaign begins in the fall, when letters are sent out to every resident of the La Cañada Flintridge School District asking for contributions. (See sample letters at the end of the chapter.) A typical letter to "friends and neighbors" states: "For years . . . residents have benefitted from the high property values which reflect the excellent reputation of our school district. We don't want this to change."

The foundation approaches local businesses directly asking for donations. In addition, many businesses match contributions made by their employees, and SOS distributes to donors a brochure listing businesses that have matched donations in the past. While many of these businesses include the corporations you might expect to see on such a list—Mobil, Coca-Cola, and Hughes Aircraft, for instance—even some smaller businesses match contributions. "One tiny insurance firm matches donations up to $500," says Lettice Carroll.

On back-to-school night, a pitch is made in every classroom for parents to contribute, and a parent representative in each classroom at the elementary school level follows up with a written request to fellow parents. About 30 percent of parents responded to the plea in a recent school year, for a combined contribution of $40,000. (Elementary enrollment is 2,000.)

In December, another letter goes out reminding people that they can still make a contribution and take a tax deduction for the current calendar year. The foundation is set up as a 501(c)(3) nonprofit corporation, so contributions are deductible for purposes of the federal income tax.

In the winter and spring, the foundation sponsors a black-tie dinner/silent auction and a jogathon. Recently, the dinner, attended by 370 people, raised over $40,000.

In May, another letter requests donations and itemizes things the district would buy with the money raised. This list is drawn up by the school district's administration, which works closely with SOS. "We find if we name some things that donations would buy, people are a little more willing to contribute," says Lettice Carroll.

Over the summer, names of people who contributed to the foundation over the past school year are published in a brochure and a community newspaper. Donors are listed by categories indicating the size of the donation:

Golden Circle: $2,000 or more

Benefactor: $1,000 to $1,999

Patron: $500 to $999

Honor Roll: $200 to $499

Supporter: up to $199

Donors can elect to remain anonymous by checking off a box on their pledge cards. (A sample pledge card appears at the end of the chapter.)

Although SOS began on a small scale in 1978, it is now a well-organized and highly efficient operation. It buys mailing lists and publishes professional-looking brochures, including a fourteen-page question-and-answer booklet. (A sample page appears at the end of the chapter.)

ADVERTISEMENTS IN JOURNALS AND SCHOOL DIRECTORIES

For many years, private schools have raised considerable sums by selling advertising space in school directories and programs or "journals" of major social events. Public schools are beginning to look to this approach as a major source of funds.

School Directories

A 450-student school in Virginia nets about $4,000 annually after expenses from its school directory. Each child and teacher receives one free copy of the directory, which is like a telephone book for school families. "Families can purchase a second copy for a few dollars, and many do so to have an extra copy by an upstairs telephone. The directory is like a Bible. Kids and parents love it," says the PTA president, Susan Ricci.

The directory gives complete class lists and separately an alphabetical listing of each family that agrees to have its address and phone number published. Names of faculty, other staff, and PTA executive board members also appear. The back pages of the directory are devoted to ads.

Fifth- and sixth-graders compete in a contest to design the directory's front cover. The inside front cover of one year's directory displays a full-page ad, and the dedication page clearly states: "This directory is for the sole use of the families and staff of _____ School and is not to be used for solicitations of any kind."

How does the directory raise money if it's distributed free to all students? By contributing $10, parents become sponsors and have their names listed as such in the directory. Local businesses and businesses run by parents purchase advertising space in the directory:

$12 for business-card size

$30 for one-fourth of a page

$50 for one-half of a page

$100 for a full page

The first day of school, students go home with a form to fill out for the directory (see the sample at the end of the chapter). The form asks for the information to be published in the directory, permission to print it, and donations in its support. Families that haven't returned their fliers after a week or two get a follow-up letter (see the sample at the end of the chapter), and those who don't respond to that letter get telephone calls. Meanwhile, a small committee geographically divvies up the area surrounding the school, and volunteers approach businesses asking them to purchase advertising space. Most of the people taking out ads are parents who have businesses, such as realtors, piano teachers, doctors, and lawyers.

The dedication page of the directory collectively thanks all the advertisers. Martha Harris, chair of the directory one year, says that she believes it's important for advertisers to be thanked personally. She enclosed a copy of the dedication page with the thank-you that she wrote to each advertiser.

A school in New Jersey held a sock hop for parents and teachers and earned $5,000 from a journal published for the occasion. Advertising rates ranged from $100 for a full-page ad to $15 for a business-card ad and $10 for name only. A committee of thirty people was formed to solicit ads, and each member received a letter setting out guidelines for solicitation. (See the sample at the end of the chapter).

Parents were encouraged to take out ads themselves, either for their businesses or just as families wishing the school well. (A sample flier asking for ads appears at the end of the chapter.) A father wrote letters to each of 100 fathers who had attended a breakfast with the principal earlier in the year. (A letter like this appears at the end of the chapter.)

One particularly industrious mother wrote letters to everyone who had done work for her—her plumber, electrician, dentist, doctor—asking them to take out ads. She explained that if they didn't have camera-ready ads or typeset copy, they could simply send in their business cards, which could be blown up to any size, or write messages on their stationery. She enclosed an application for an ad and a self-addressed envelope and said that she got positive responses from about half of the people to whom she'd written. (A sample letter and application form appear at the end of the chapter.)

BUSINESS CONTRIBUTIONS

Space doesn't allow a complete enumeration of the many ways in which businesses have been helping public schools, especially in recent years. This section simply highlights a few of the ways in which the business community can provide direct financial support to schools.

Grocery Store Programs

GIFT CERTIFICATES

Some grocery stores have programs whereby schools sell gift certificates (scrip) that parents can use to pay for purchases at the supermarket. The schools get to keep a percentage of sales—usually around 5 percent. Since everybody needs to buy groceries, the potential profit is substantial.

Although it seems as if this would be an effortless way to raise a lot of money, think carefully about how to distribute the gift certificates, which are like cash. Don't risk losing them in the mail or in children's backpacks.

RECEIPTS FOR CASH

A grocery store in Wyoming has a program called Dollars for the Students. As shoppers leave the store, they deposit their receipts into the bin labeled with the name of their school. At the end of six months, the grocery store donates to the schools a total of $10,000, divided up according to the percentage of sales in each bin. For instance, if the receipts in one school's bin totaled 3.5 percent of total sales in all the bins, that school would get $350 (3.5 percent of $10,000). "Last year, we earned $324," says Pauline Griess, "which we thought was great. The employees of the store did all the work of adding the receipts— another plus!"

LABELS AND RECEIPTS

Some companies have programs whereby schools collect product labels or receipts from participating grocery stores and fast-food restaurants and redeem them for school equipment and supplies. Apple Computer and IBM sponsored programs of this sort for several years and put thousands of computers in schools around the country.

"We participated in the IBM and Apple receipt programs and over two years built an entire computer lab at school. It was great," says one mom. "However, we did have some concerns over the impression that we were 'endorsing' products or stores. After all, some parents worked at rival stores not offering receipt programs."

An ambitious mother in Delaware organized a massive effort in her school to collect labels under three different programs. Her school of 350 students collected receipts and labels worth $85,000 from one grocery store, $83,000 from another, and 6,000 labels from Campbell's, Prego, Pepperidge Farm, Swanson, Marie's, and Mrs. Paul's products.

About 70,000 schools participate in the Campbell's label program every year. Some schools don't participate because it requires so many labels to earn supplies: 800 labels for a basketball, 1,400 for a globe, and 80,000 for a personal computer, for instance.

On the other hand, collecting grocery receipts and labels has the advantage that it can be done by everyone at school, regardless of economic status. Only when she began totaling grocery receipts did the Delaware mom, Lynn Fornadel, realize how many school families paid for groceries with food stamps. She believes that these programs provide a way for less-affluent families to support the school, since they wouldn't be in the position of being able to buy expensive wrapping paper or food products if the school sold them as fund-raisers.

At the very beginning, read the program's instructions on how to collect labels—which parts to save, how to cut them, and how to bundle them. "One program required that 100 labels be banded together, another called for 500 to be tied together with string. I had some rework to do at the end, because I had not read all the instructions," says Lynn Fornadel.

Send home detailed instructions to parents so that they know which labels to collect and how to send them in to school. Here is what Lynn Fornadel did: "I sent out a hand-written letter, because I felt it put me on more of a personal basis with the parents. On a separate sheet, I wrote an alphabetical listing of all labels to save and asked everyone to post the list in the kitchen. About once a month, I sent out a reminder to the parents and also a progress report. I made a cover for a big can at school, wrapped it in bright yellow, and drew a train on it filled with cars of labels and cans. The train was going up a big hill and on the other side was our goal 'station.' Our motto was 'I think we can, I know we CAN!!!' I tried to keep up with the cutting and not to let it pile up. This was very important."

Adopt-a-School Programs

Around the country, businesses are "adopting" schools, donating goods, cash, and employee time. The Adopt-a-School Program in Cheyenne, Wyoming, is fairly typical of these programs. Each school in the district is adopted by one or two local businesses, such as banks, car dealers, life insurance companies, restaurants, hospitals, and county offices. The program is flexible, and each business helps its school in a somewhat different way.

A bank adopted one of Cheyenne's elementary schools and did the following:

✎ presented each student citizen of the month with a balloon and pencil (at an assembly or in the classroom)

✎ gave a $50 savings bond to an outstanding student (selected by the faculty) each quarter

✎ sponsored an ice cream sundae party for a top-selling class at the end of a fund-raiser

✎ placed large cans in the bank lobby for employees and customers to deposit labels for Campbell's label program

✎ displayed children's artwork in the bank

✎ donated employee time so that the school got one hour of volunteer time every day throughout the year (The volunteer would report to the school office and be assigned wherever needed on a particular day)

ALUMNI CONTRIBUTIONS

The simplest way to solicit donations from alumni is to contact them directly by phone or mail. Some schools invite alumni to their clothesline sales, and many invite them to social events at school that double as fund-raisers.

A FINAL THOUGHT

Although fund-raising should never be the sole or even chief concern of the PTA, nearly every school does some fund-raising over the course of the year. Armed with the ideas in this book, you should be able to take a fresh look at your own fund-raising. Remember that your objective is to improve the educational program and build a stronger sense of community within your school family—in short, to make your school a better place for children to learn and grow.

—✱——✱——✱—

Together We Can Grow

PTA Membership Drive

Dear Parents:

Become a member of the PTA, and together we can make dreams for the future start to grow. By showing your support for Lincoln School, your name will be added to our Wall of Recognition, which will be growing daily. Each class with 100 percent participation will have a Sno-Kone Day.

Joining PTA demonstrates your commitment to your child's education and ensures the overall continued excellence provided to our students. The PTA membership fee is $3.25 per person and $6.50 per family.

PTA Direct Contribution Program

This year we are going to try something new. Over the past few years there has been a growing interest in direct contributions. The PTA is inviting families and businesses wishing to make a contribution to do so beginning with the kick-off of our PTA Membership Drive. Seventy-five percent of all contributions will go directly into our children's classroom. The remaining 25 percent will continue to go toward already established programs sponsored by our PTA.

Why You Should Contribute

Our initial goal with the Direct Contribtuion Program is to at least match the funds that the district allots for instructional supplies for each child at our school, which is approximately $23 per child. If each family were to match these funds, think of the IMPACT! For example, a contribution of $25 per student would have a positive impact on our student body of approximately $11,250. Matching funds would allow a more efficient and effective use of not only monies but also people (both professional and volunteer) in each classroom.

(continued)

Your tax-deductible contribution can be made on a onetime basis, semiannually, quarterly, or monthly. So the options on a $25 contribution would be as follows:

One time	$25.00	Quarterly	$6.25
Semiannually	$12.50	Monthly	$2.50

It is our hope that with the direct contributions and three major fund-raisers (PTA Membership Drive, Gift Wrap Program, and the Knowledge-a-thon), budgeting and funding decisions can be made sooner and our volunteers' hours will be more effective. Please make all checks payable to the Lincoln School PTA. All direct contributions will also be highlighted on our Wall of Recognition. Should you have any questions, please contact our PTA membership chairperson or either of our PTA presidents.

PTA Membership Chairperson

Yes, we _____ wish to contribute $ _____ to the PTA Direct Contribution Program.

Name and room number of each child:

_____

_____

_____

Please circle your contribution option:

One time (September or October)
Semiannually (October and January)
Quarterly (September, January, April, June)
Monthly (September thru June)

**EDUCATIONAL
FOUNDATION**

Dear Friends and Neighbors:

Our community schoolchildren need your help. Inadequate state funding and the failure of the parcel tax have left our schools short more than $1.2 million this year. As the school year begins, we write to ask for your much-needed financial support for our local schools.

For years, _____ residents have benefitted from the high property values which reflect the excellent reputation of our school district. We don't want this to change.

Like all California public schools, the _____ public schools receive approximately 90 percent of their funds from the state. Each year, these state funds purchase fewer and fewer educational services and materials, and today California's public schools are among the most poorly funded in the nation! Our children deserve better. To better understand the severity and consequences of this situation, please read the enclosed brochure.

Within our community, there is widespread determination to provide high-quality public education despite the difficulties in Sacramento. Thirteen years ago, the _____ Educational Foundation was established to harness the commitment of our citizens and businesses to our local schools. Since then, contributions of more than $3 million have been donated to provide important educational opportunities for thousands of children. Such funds are needed more urgently this year than ever before.

Please be generous. Your special tax-deductible gift of $100, $250, $500, or more will make a difference in this vital campaign. Of course, *any* amount is greatly appreciated!

Many employers will match funds donated to the Educational Foundation. Check with your company. A matched gift can double your contribution.

Help our children. Help save our schools. Help maintain property values. It's up to us, *all* of us . . . For Kids' Sake. Thank you in advance for your generous donation.

Sincerely,

EDUCATIONAL FOUNDATION

Dear Parents:

Thank you for your continued support of our schools in these difficult financial times.

Even though a large majority (62 percent) of citizens voted yes on the recent parcel tax election to help fund our local schools, we did not reach the two-thirds vote required for passing California tax measures.

That's why we need the tax-deductible gifts from you and your friends and neighbors *now* more than ever. Your child's future depends on you. There is no one else.

As a community we must rally around the needs of our community's greatest asset, our public schools.

The goal of $500,000 previously set for this year covers our pledge to the school district for money already budgeted for *this* school year. But without the guarantee of additional funds, our school district cannot budget money for teachers, remedial services, textbooks, or instructional supplies for the *next* school year. This means that without more money, class sizes will go up and the academic program will be further eroded.

That is why the _____ Educational Foundation has raised its goal to $1,700,000. To reach this goal, we must have 100 percent participation by our school parents and everyone else who feels strongly about the importance of quality public schools for our community, our children, and our nation.

It will be extremely challenging to raise privately the $1.2 million each year that the parcel tax would have raised, plus the amount pledged yearly by _____. However, it is not impossible.

Please take advantage of a tax deduction before the end of the year and make a gift today. If every school family donated $700 to _____ this year, we would make our goal. Compared to the cost of private schools, this is a bargain. If you can increase your gift now, please do it. But give what you can. Any amount will be appreciated.

Thank you for supporting outstanding schools.

Sincerely,

_____

SAMPLE PLEDGE CARD

Donor Group
_____ Business
_____ Realtor
_____ Professional
_____ Grandparents/relatives

Name (owner/manager) _____

Name of business _____
                    (as it will appear in local publications)

Address _____

Phone _____
                    I wish to remain anonymous. ☐

Yes, I want to make a donation.
My tax-deductible contribution for this year's campaign is: $_____

Golden Circle	$2,000 or more	**Honor Roll**	$200 to $499
Benefactor	$1,000 to $1,999	**Supporter**	up to $199
Patron	$500 to $999		

We enclose $_____ for our total donation.
We enclose $_____ for one-half of our donation.
We pledge $_____ to be paid in _____ number of installments.

Total contribution due by _____

☐ I will request **matching funds** from my employer.
☐ I wish to volunteer to help on this year's campaign.

Make your tax-deductible check payable to
_____ **Educational Foundation.**
Your check is your receipt.

SAMPLE PAGE FROM BROCHURE

FOR KIDS' SAKE!

WHAT IS _____ ?

_____ is a private charitable foundation devoted to maintaining and improving the schools of _____ . It is not a part of, nor is it affiliated with, the School Board. It is staffed entirely by volunteers. It is formally known as the ___ Educational Foundation.

WHAT IS THE PURPOSE OF _____ ?

_____ raises funds through purely voluntary donations which are donated to the _____ School District and used to maintain and improve the quality of education in the public schools.

WHAT ARE ITS GOALS?

The short-term goal of _____ is to provide funds to the school district to allow the schools to attempt to maintain current programs. Given current funding shortfalls, *our goal is to help the district simply "hold the line."* The long-term goal is to assist in providing funds sufficient to significantly reduce class sizes, broaden program offerings, and add an additional class period at the high school level.

WE HAVE A SERIOUS PROBLEM

WHY DO _____ SCHOOLS NEED ADDITIONAL FUNDS?

The answer is unfortunately very simple. *Revenues are not keeping pace with increases in costs.* As discussed in more detail below, numerous programs have been cut from the current year's budget. Despite these cutbacks, the _____ school costs will still increase by 1.9 percent. However, revenues (including this year's _____ pledge) will only increase by 0.1 percent. This 1.8 percent difference will result in a deficit for this year alone in excess of $50,000. In past years the shortfall based on this factor has been even greater. For instance, in _____ the shortfall was over $500,000. This fact has forced the district to use reserves to maintain programs.

WHAT HAS BEEN THE IMPACT OF THESE SHORTFALLS OVER THE YEARS?

Numerous programs have been cut from the budget. Class size has increased dramatically in the last several years (an average increase of four students per class per year for the last two years). Remedial classes in reading and math have been eliminated. The advanced placement/honors program for college preparation has been altered dramatically. Maintenance and janitorial services have been eliminated or reduced. Many extracurricular activities and sports programs have been cut.

SAMPLE REMINDER NOTICE

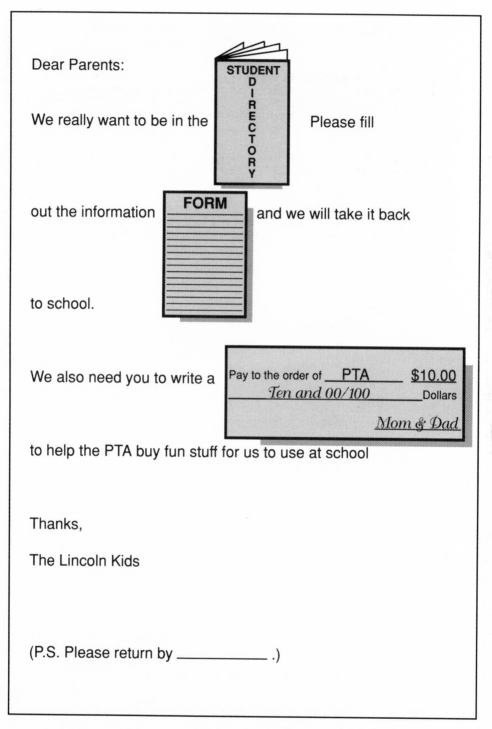

Dear Parents:

We really want to be in the **STUDENT DIRECTORY** Please fill

out the information **FORM** and we will take it back

to school.

We also need you to write a Pay to the order of ___ PTA ___ $10.00
Ten and 00/100 Dollars
Mom & Dad

to help the PTA buy fun stuff for us to use at school

Thanks,

The Lincoln Kids

(P.S. Please return by _____ .)

Dear Parents:

On Saturday, November 1, Lincoln School's PTA will be sponsoring an evening of mystery and swinging to Music of the Fifties and Sixties provided by a local DJ. All profits will be for the benefit of the school playground. Help make this event a success by taking out your own personal ad in the evening's journal.

Your "ad" can be a good-luck message to the school, your name, or anything else you feel you'd like to say in one line (twenty-six characters).

The cost to place a personal ad is $10. The value to the school is priceless. Please fill out the form on the bottom of this page and return to school before _____ . We have also listed the cost of larger ads for those who are so inclined. Thank you!!

Cochairs, Fund-raising

I would like to help Lincoln School's playground fund by placing a personal ad (no longer than twenty-six characters, please) in the Murder at the Sock Hop Journal. I would like my ad to read:

_____

_____

_____

I enclose $10 per one-line ad. Child's name and room number _____

_____

Prices for additional ads:

$100 for a full page ad
$50 for one-half of a page
$25 for one-quarter of a page
$15 for business-card size

Name _____

Address _____

Business name _____

Size of ad and price _____

Phone _____

Please make all checks payable to Lincoln School PTA.

Dear "_____ 100" Father:

One hundred of us gathered together last fall with one thing in common . . . the desire to participate in some way in our child's education. Now there is a very substantial way to help our children and future generations. This may be our chance to leave a lasting mark.

Lincoln School needs a first-class playground . . . one that will exercise both the bodies and minds of the children who use it. We, the fathers, can make it happen. As part of the PTA-sponsored "Sock Hop" on Saturday night, November 1, there is going to be a journal/program.

We have two important jobs!!

1. Attend the party and have a good time.

2. Support the project's success with an ad, full page if you can.

An ad form is attached. We ask that you return it by _____ . Thanks in advance for your participation.

Sincerely,

_____

P.S. If you don't have a typeset ad available, just use your personal or business stationery to type a letter of support for inclusion in the journal.

SAMPLE LETTER TO POTENTIAL ADVERTISERS

Dear _____ :

I am presently working on a journal for a fund-raiser for my daughter's school, _____ . While looking through my business cards, I came across yours. My husband and I felt that since we've used your services before, perhaps you'd like to advertise to other _____ residents through this journal. This could be helpful for you in obtaining new business and for us to raise monies for a much needed playground for the school.

I have enclosed an application for an ad along with a self-addressed envelope. If you do not have a camera-ready ad or typeset copy, you can use your business card (blown up to any size), or you could write a message on your personal or business stationery.

The deadline to get this in is _____ . If I can answer any questions you might have, please feel free to call me at _____ .

I appreciate your consideration on _____ 's behalf.

Sincerely,

Vice President—PTA
Fund-raising

APPLICATION FOR ADVERTISEMENT JOURNAL

Prices: $100 for a full page ad
          50 for one-half of a page
          25 for one-quarter of a page
          15 for business-card size
          10 for name only

Name _____

Address _____

Business name _____

Size of ad and price _____

Phone _____

Please make your check payable to the _____ PTA—Journal, and return application form and check to the PTA box at school.

Re: Sock Hop Dance
    Advertising Journal

Dear Committee Member:

Thank you for your commitment to work with us on our advertising journal that will be handed out at our February Sock Hop. The following is a list of guidelines to be used when asking for participation.

1. _____ wants to make sure that this effort does not conflict with our future fund-raising for the Fun Fair, so we must make sure that we do *not* approach the same vendors that we use for the raffle prizes.

2. The best prospective advertisers will be your friends, family, spouses, business associates, lawyers, beauticians, etc., and any other vendors outside of _____ .

3. The prices of the ads are as follows:
    $100 for a full page
    $50 for one-half of a page
    $25 for one-fourth of a page
    $15 for business-card size
    $10 for name only

4. All ads must be "camera ready." The people you approach will usually know what that means and will probably have an advertisement "mechanical" in their files. If not, they can get one ready or ask us to help them with it, or we could blow up a business card to the size ad they buy.

5. Checks should be made payable to the _____ PTA—Journal. The ads and checks should be put in the PTA box at school to the attention of _____ .

Enclosed are ten applications for your immediate use. If you need more, please contact _____ at _____ .

Thank you for your cooperation and effort on our school's behalf, and good luck!!!

                                        Sincerely,

                                        Vice President—PTA
                                        Fund-raising
                                        Cochairs—Sock Hop

INDEX